For You

Andreas Seidl

Handover of Power

Global Version

Volume 18: Justice

Imprint

Bibliographic information of the German National Library:
The German National Library lists this publication in the
German National Bibliography; detailed bibliographic data
are available on the Internet at http://dnb.dnb.de.

© 2022 Dipl. Pol. Theodor Andreas Seidl

Cover: Christiane Ebrecht
Translation: DeepL, Cologne
Production and publishing: BoD – Books on Demand,
Norderstedt

ISBN: 978-3-7562-9441-1

Acknowledgements

My thanks go to my family and friends who have made me who I am today. Special thanks to all those who supported me in writing this book. I would like to thank all my classmates, teachers, fellow students, lecturers, demonstrators, activists, colleagues, companies and countries with whom I have had the privilege of sharing the experiences from which all the ideas in this book have emerged. I would like to thank the staff of Books on Demand for their kind helpfulness. I thank the citizens of Seligenstadt for the harmony and solidarity in which I was able to write.

Foreword

This policy concept contains a variety of proposals for possible political reforms. It can be peacefully and democratically adapted to any current political system of any state in the world, but also to political systems in families, clubs, associations or companies. Wherever humans make or submit to rules that manage living together, the following proposals can be helpful. Readers who find the proposals so helpful that they would like to implement them together with like-minded people can contact the author. The contact form on the last page can be used for this purpose.

Faults and defects
I ask for your understanding that this volume was not professionally proofread. I could only afford professional proofreading for the summary. Spelling errors and unfortunate phrasing may therefore occur. As soon as this volume has sold enough to pay for a professional proofreading, it will be done. After that, a new edition will be published.

English version
Please understand that this volume has been translated automatically. I could only afford a professional translation for the summary. Poor wording and spelling errors may therefore occur. In case of doubt, the German version shall prevail. As soon as this volume has sold enough to pay for a professional translation, it will be done. After that, a new edition will be

published. It was more important to me that no one in the world should have an information advantage than individual translation errors in the complete work.

References
If something has been quoted directly, it is set in italics. If the headings contain footnotes, the sources for direct and indirect quotations apply in the chapter for which the heading stands. Otherwise, quotations or source references are directly at the word or at the end of the sentence or paragraph. This book contains parts of text based on the Federal Constitution of the Swiss Confederation of 18 April 1999 (as of 12 February 2017), abbreviated to BV[1] and the Constitution of the Canton of Bern of 6 June 1993 (as of 11 March 2015), abbreviated to KV[2] .

If the constitutional paragraph, or individual paragraphs thereof, are based in whole or in part on extracts from the BV or KV, this is indicated in a footnote. The references to the corresponding footnotes for constitutional paragraphs are usually found after the heading of the affected chapter and sometimes in the body of the text. Articles used in the Swiss constitutions are listed in the footnote with a number after the title of the constitutional paragraph. Example: §123 Sample title: BV Art.123, KV Art.123.

All internet sources are fully cited in the footnotes. They were last accessed on 30.09.2021. All literature sources are also listed in full in the footnotes.

All references to tasks undertaken by other ministries and described in more detail there are given in footnotes. Example: Model Ministry - 1.2.3 Model Chapter.

All footnotes are to be viewed in comparison to the respective source, so-called indirect quotations. Direct quotations are set in italics, but hardly ever occur. The source reference is intended to enable further investigation and to take copyright

---

1 This is not an official publication. Only the publication by the Swiss Federal Chancellery is authoritative. https://www.fedlex.admin.ch/eli/cc/1999/404/de On 14.12.2021

2 This is not an official publication. The Bernese Official Collection of Laws is authoritative. https://www.belex.sites.be.ch/frontend/versions/2420?locale=de#ART71 On 16.12.2021

into account.

Table of contents

1 Goals of the Ministry of Justice

The Ministry of Justice aims to provide the people with a legally secure environment in which citizens gain confidence in the justice of the applicable norms. The Ministry of Justice ensures retribution when injustice is reported and also ensures that such injustice is not repeated in the future, if the unclear legal situation is to blame. In this way, it takes away the fear of being treated unjustly by the state or fellow human beings, or of having to live in fear of revenge.

As part of the judiciary, the Ministry of Justice aims to be the judicial power in the state, which has an undivided monopoly among the ministries for this purpose. It can discipline other ministries and citizens to comply with the applicable norms through sentences. The Ministry of Justice aims to create forms of punishment that are capable of parenting offenders into non-punitive humans and treating psychological damage in offenders and victims.

Through its funding methods, the ministry aims to achieve the goal of cost recovery or 10% profit margin. Connected to the goal of cost recovery or profit financing of the administration of justice and the penal system is the goal of motivating the people towards justice. By making certain areas of law Tax-funded, it makes sense for citizens to behave justly or not let injustice happen in order to reduce taxes. In the penal system, prisoners usually work on major projects for the state. In this way, they morally excuse themselves to society because they make up for their damage through their benefit.

2 Departments

The departments are divided into sub-departments and enumerations are usually considered as their individual units. Many tasks of some departments are completely taken over by other ministries as a service.

2.1 Central Department

Part of the Central Department is the reception office with the courier and mail room, which directs all concerns, broadcasts and visitors to the appropriate place in the ministry.

2.1.1 Staff

The Human Resources Department is responsible for staff development and planning. For this purpose, it takes care of the recruitment of junior staff, intern and trainee programmes as well as the selection procedures for employees and special selection procedures for applicants with disabilities. For politicians and employees, the department prepares a job plan. In all its tasks, it works in voting with the personnel board.[1]

All other personnel matters are transferred to the respective ministries. The Ministry of Education is responsible for the training and further education of employees for the state service.[2] The Ministry of Labour takes over the service law.[3] This includes the labour and collective bargaining law for employees in the state service, remuneration, personnel administration of all careers and employees, flexitime, holiday and sickness records, working time with or without flexitime in part-time or full-time at the place of work or in home work. The Ministry of Infrastructure provides housing assistance for all state employees.[4] The Ministry of Finance's Pay Office takes care of employees' salary, expenses, travel and relocation costs.[5]

The Ministry of Education provides childcare for all employees in the state service.[6]

The Ministry of Health is responsible for the occupational health service.[7] It ensures occupational health management,

---

1 Ministry of State Organisation - 2.1.1.1 Personnel board
2 Ministry of Education - 2.1.1.1 Education and training for the state service
3 Ministry of Labour - 4 State enterprises, 13 Labour Directory
4 Ministry of Infrastructure - 2.1.1.1 Housing assistance for state service employees
5 Ministry of Finance - 2.1.1.1 Staff remuneration
6 Ministry of Education - 2.1.1.2 Childcare for state service employees
7 Ministry of Health - 2.1.1.1 Occupational Health Service

deals with the treatment, education and prevention of occupational accidents, controls and provides occupational health and safety through the health auditors[8] of the Company Auditing Agency[9] .

2.1.2 Organisation

The ministries of media, justice, finance, labour, state organisation provide audit services for quality management in the ministry, evaluation of work performance, revenues and expenditures, as well as prevention of corruption, protection against sabotage and, if necessary, disciplinary matters.[10]
The Ministry of Labour regulates procurement law and ensures corruption-free state orders and procurement.[11] The Ministry of Finance organises the annual budget vote and ensures proper accounting in each ministry.[12] It regulates budget procedures, budget law, staff budgets, departmental budgets, costs and cash management, and assists ministries in budget planning for the budget vote. The language service for translating talks or texts is provided by the Ministry of Education.[13]
The Ministry of Digital Affairs supports the supply of Information Technology.[14] In voting with the Procurement Office of the Ministry of Labour, it takes care of the procurement, provision, maintenance and service of technical devices and software. Much of this is produced in-house to ensure data protection in information and communication technology. Information technology and digitalisation officers audit and advise the ministries. Digital appointment calendar and documentation services are provided as well as a digital policy archive including a library.

---

8 Ministry of Labour - 20.7.2 Health auditor
9 Ministry of Labor - 20 Company Auditing Agency
10 Ministries of Media, Security, Justice, Finance, State Organisation - 2.1.2.1 Audit services
11 Ministry of Labour - 6 Procurement Office
12 Ministry of Finance - 8 state revenues, 9 state expenditure
13 Ministry of Education - 2.1.3 Language Service
14 Ministry of Digital Affairs - 2.1.2.1.1 Supply of Information Technology

2.1.2.1 Audit services

The Jurisprudence and Prison Departments provide independent review of courts and prisons and receive complaints from participants. The Public Prosecutor's Office of the National Court of Justice is empowered as an independent audit service to investigate and prosecute state institutions.

2.2 Management Department

The Management Department is the minister's department. With his office team, he provides policy planning and analysis for his ministry and coordinates the relationship between the nation and the municipality through exchanges with his deputies in the municipalities. He initiates cooperation with other ministries or citizens in committees and is supported by the Ministry of State Organisation.

The Ministry of Media Affairs, through its media service, provides press and public relations for the ministry, moderates civil dialogue, trains or provides a spokesperson for the minister, writes speeches and texts on request, and ensures the implementation of conferences and events.[15]

The Ministry of Digital Affairs is responsible for digital management and thus provides departmental management. It automatically produces business statistics, staff surveys and the current state of research through statistics. It automatically forwards proposals to the affected or empowered state employees. In document management, it ensures digitalisation and that ministries share forms with each other.[16]

2.3 Foreign Department

The Foreign Department regulates all intergovernmental and international legal proceedings.

---

15 Ministry of Media Affairs - 2.2.1.1 Media Service
16 Ministry of Digital Affairs - 2.1.2.1 Digital Service

2.3.1 International jurisdiction

In voting with the Ministry of Foreign Affairs, the Ministry of Justice determines the responsibility of international courts and their jurisprudence in accordance with applicable international law. The Ministry of Foreign Affairs ensures the participation of the nation in the creation and implementation of international law in cooperation with the United Nations[17] . The law of international law and international treaties is pronounced in national courts, unless international courts have been created for this purpose. All international courts must be subject to the law of the international organisations that operate them. If there are no such international organisations, the Ministry of Justice, in voting with the Ministry of Foreign Affairs, is responsible for drafting, in cooperation with the affected states, rules governing the responsibility and functioning of the international courts to be created.

2.3.2 International law enforcement

In international law enforcement, the Ministry of Foreign Affairs, in voting with the Ministry of Justice, facilitates cooperation with the responsible foreigner security and justice authorities and international courts. This primarily involves cooperation in the area of legal assistance, for example for the taking of evidence, as well as in the area of enforcement assistance, for example through the extradition of offenders who are considered criminals in both states. International civil procedural law, private international law and international conflicts in child matters, are implemented within the framework of possible interstate legal assistance that both affected states can agree on. The Ministry of Foreign Affairs also takes care of the necessary negotiations with the foreigner. An international central register of criminal offences is being set up with the security agencies of foreign countries, primarily to combat terrorism and organised gang crime internationally. Cases in the area of international criminal law and international criminal law are conducted under international criminal

---

17https://www.un.org/en/

procedure law by the International Criminal Court.

2.3.2.1 Extradition requests[18]

Foreign states can submit extradition requests to the Ministry of Foreign Affairs for persons who have committed a criminal offence in their foreign country and subsequently entered the inland in order to evade prosecution. If the offence is not a criminal offence inland, the extradition request will not be approved. If the person is not a domestic citizens, he or she is granted asylum in the national territory. If, however, he or she commits a crime inland, he or she will be deported to the foreign country of which he or she is a national.

The responsible court works with the Ministry of Foreign Affairs to file extradition requests abroad if offenders have fled abroad. However, the judge can also impose a life-long entry ban and confiscate any property of the offender remaining inland.

2.4 Lawmaking Department

The Lawmaking Department takes care of the implementation of the principles of the rule of law and organises cooperation with the other ministries. In cooperation with the minister, legislation is made for the criminal law of the Ministry of Justice. The department also ensures that all existing constitutional articles and laws are properly divided into the various areas of law. The Law Directory is operated by this department and the profiles and groups of all norms are categorised according to the ladder of norms.

2.5 Jurisprudence Department

The Jurisprudence Department organises the administration of justice in the courts. This includes the proper conduct of all court proceedings according to the same standards, an

---

18§24 Protection against expulsion, extradition and deportation: BV Art.25

appropriate assessment of damages, as well as the uniform requirements for court staff and their corresponding remuneration. The department operates the Court Directory and verifies the completeness of all proceedings and judgements as well as their anonymisation and publication.

2.6 Prison Department

The Prison Department is responsible for the administration of clemency law and the various forms of punishment. It administers the coffers of all courts for monetary fines and compensation payments. In cooperation with the Ministries of Labour and Economy, it monitors compliance with occupational bans. In cooperation with the Ministry of Planned Economy, it agrees on the areas of activity for community service and establishes contact between the relevant Social Village and the appropriate court. In cooperation with all ministries, occupational activities are selected for prisoners with different qualifications in state institutions and private companies, and contact is established between prisons and workplaces. Prisoners can contact the department if they wish to voice complaints about prison conditions or open court proceedings, for example to have their case newly heard or to request prison privileges.

3 Tasks of the Ministry of Justice

The central task of the Ministry of Justice is to enact laws for the rule of law and to create institutions, such as courts and prisons, in which these procedures can be implemented. This also includes recruiting judicial and prison staff, regularising their working practices and ensuring that they are fairly remunerated.

The ministry's tasks include organising cooperation with all other ministries and citizens. All other ministries must coordinate penal laws with the Ministry of Justice to ensure proportionality in comparison with all other penal laws. When laws need to be renewed after a revision case, the Ministry of Justice sends the orders to the affected ministries with a deadline for processing. If ministries have tasks that could be done by prisoners, they report this to the Ministry of Justice, which arranges for prisoners to take over the work, provided the effort does not exceed the wages.

Cooperation with the Ministry of Security is closest because the security agencies participate in the collection of evidence and bring offenders to justice.

Cooperation with citizens takes place through citizens filing complaints, engaging as lay judges, appearing in court as defendants or witnesses, and as convicted persons having to implement the sentences ordered. In addition to court proceedings, the Ministry of Justice enables citizens to oversee the work of judges and prosecutors through the Court Directory and provide a decision-making tool for the election of judges. Through the Law Directory, citizens can take on the work of searching for norms in need of reform and opening a repeal quorum. All directly elected politicians of the Ministry of Justice, including judges, are elected according to the election of persons process determined by the Ministry of State Organisation.[19]

The Ministry of Justice leads the cooperation with companies by looking for suitable companies, by having companies report to it to be screened for suitability, and by selecting suitable prisons and prisoners to complete agreed orders.

4 Principles of the rule of law

The principles of the rule of law are based on five principles. In the handling of law, i.e. in the drafting, executive and jurisprudence of constitutional articles, laws and further norms such as court judgments, these principles must be observed. They consist of predictability, transparency, legal certainty, proportionality and impartiality.

---

19 Ministry of State Organisation - 9.9 Elections of persons

4.1 Predictability[20]

Laws must be known. They are accessible to all citizens via the Law Directory. In addition, the Ministry of Digital Affairs offers the Algoracle[21] to simulate actions for compliance with the law.

The state behaves predictably because its actions are always based on norms that are adapted to the conditions in the country and with which the majority of the population agrees. If the state wants to adapt its actions to the prevailing or future conditions, it must first obtain the consent of the population. Citizens and companies act predictably because their actions and plans are shaped by the constitution and the laws that follow from it. For other states, actions of nations and municipalities are predictable because they abide by international law.

4.2 Transparency[22]

Laws must be comprehensible. Via the Law Directory, citizens can see who enacted the law, when and by which majority, and which judge used it in which proceedings to approve or disapprove a particular case.

Constitutional articles and laws protect citizens from arbitrary state action because all state agencies must know and apply them. If state arbitrariness nevertheless takes place, citizens can file complaints against security agencies at various points.

4.3 Legal certainty[23]

Laws must be reliable. Laws are valid only from the day on which they appear in the Law Directory. Retroactive convictions for acts are inadmissible. This applies to offences that are time-barred and to acts that were not punishable before the date of publication of the law.

---

20 §54,1-4 Principles of the rule of law: BV Art.5
21 Ministry of Digital Affairs - 15.3 Algoracle
22 §3,1,3 Protection against state arbitrariness: BV Art.9
23 §54,5,6 Principles of the rule of law: KV Art.26

The inheritance of guilt is also inadmissible. The person or generation causing the debt is at fault. Liability for personal fault cannot be transferred to any other person. The social liability, which has arisen through the voting behaviour or the omission behaviour of an entire electorate over 3 decades, cannot be transferred to the following generation.

4.4 Proportionality[24]

Sentences should be proportionate to the offence. Serious offences should be punished more severely, lighter offences more mildly, even if the same principles have been violated. Neither prosecution nor sentences should be disproportionate. Sentences and prosecution find their limits in the respect and protection of human dignity. Therefore, mental and physical torture is not permitted either for prosecution or for punishment. For the same reason, the death penalty is considered inadmissible.

4.5 Impartiality[25]

Judgments shall be rendered regardless of the biological, demographic, religious, political, ethical, ethnic, technical, national or social ancestry or opinions of the plaintiffs or defendants. Different laws for men or women are inadmissible. Different laws for disabled persons are only permissible to promote their equality. In principle, all humans are equal before the law. Unequal treatment is only permissible if the facts are unequal. Discriminatory laws may apply in cultural protection areas in order to enable a minority to maintain its segregation.[26]

24§1 Human dignity: BV Art.7, §4,1,3 Right to life: BV Art.10
25§2 Equality of rights: BV Art.8
26Ministry of Integration - 6.3 Cultural protection area

4.6 Ladder of norms

The ladder of norms describes all the types of law that humans follow to live better together. The more persons agree on ways of living that they perceive as just, the higher the norm is on the ladder of norms. Norms that are justified by democratic procedures are above other norms and give the following ranking. International norms, such as international law or continental law, are only above national norms if the sovereign state with its people recognises these rules as binding. There is no international monopoly on the use of force that could enforce compliance. The communitarisation[27] of states gradually builds up such a monopoly of force in continents and ultimately worldwide.

4.6.1 Constitution

The constitutional articles serve to define the fundamental rights and duties of humans, nationals and the state. The interaction of humans and their institutions in this country is based on these articles. All nationals are responsible for their content.

4.6.2 Laws

Laws are used by state employees as work instructions by the people and by the courts to try citizens who have broken the law. All nationals and the respective ministers are responsible for their content.

4.6.3 Court decisions

Court decisions serve as concrete examples to citizens and state employees of how the laws are applied to individual cases in accordance with the constitution. All domestic judges are responsible for their content.

------

27 Ministry of Foreign Affairs - 5 Communitarisation

4.6.4 Regulations

Regulations are used to implement laws by the executive ministries. Citizens feel these norms in the form of state services and how they are delivered. The respective ministers are responsible for their content. Each regulation must relate to at least one law.

4.6.5 Municipal laws

Municipal laws are used by local state employees as work instructions by the local population and Municipal Courts to convict citizens who have broken the law in the local area. Their content is the responsibility of all local nationals and the respective local ministers or deputy ministers in the town hall. Municipal laws provide the dynamic media democracy with the necessary flexibility for subsidiarity and federalism. From them follow locally limited effective court decisions and regulations.

4.6.6 Statutes

Statutes are used by citizens to form their own organisations and regulate the interaction between members and within their club. The members of the organisations are responsible for the content.

4.6.7 Administrative instructions

Administrative instructions are used by citizens, companies, state organisations and private organisations to document their operation as law-abiding and corruption-free. The management level of the institution to be administered is responsible for the content. Administrative instructions for state employees must be linked to a corresponding regulation.

4.6.8 Service instructions

Service instructions are used by citizens, companies, state institutions and private organisations to regulate their functioning as collaborative and expedient. Each team involved in the service is responsible for the content.

4.6.9 Habits

Habits serve humans to organise the interaction between generations and to distinguish locally or personally. A person's life course in interaction with his or her fellow human beings is responsible for the content.

4.7 Law Directory

The greatest influence of this directory is on the people's media monitoring of the executive, mediative, legislative and judiciary. Therefore, the state must clearly document how it deals with the rules of the people. In particular, this directory enables the monitoring of the laws, judgments and judges by the people.

The Law Directory contains all the norms of the ladder of norms as profiles. Each new norm adopted is given a new profile. Constitutional articles and laws are immediately linked to their filming in the Media Directory[28] . In each profile of a law, there is an overview of all areas of application in the ministries as well as of cases judicially adjudicated in which this law was applied and a link to the case in the Law Directory.

4.7.1 State profiles

The ministries publish all adopted state norms in the Law Directory, from constitutional articles to service instructions for state employees. If state norms are being drafted and have not yet been adopted, they are listed in the Legislative

---

28 Ministry of Media Affairs - 5.6 Media Directory

Directory.

Regulations, administrative instructions and service instructions for the public prosecutor's office and the police are exempt from publication if there is an investigative tactical reason. Investigative tactical reasons must be such that publication would prevent the apprehension of offenders or jeopardise the actions of the security agencies. Publication of these exceptions can be ordered in court proceedings of last resort. These proceedings must be conducted publicly so that citizens can satisfy themselves that the politicians and state employees have also implemented the existing laws in the regulations, event regulations and service instructions and have not made any deviating formulations.

4.7.2 Private profiles

Clubs publish their statutes in the Law Directory, companies their general terms and conditions. Publication is obligatory and viewing is made available to all users. Other norms of clubs and companies can only be made available to a certain group of persons.

Clubs and companies can democratically revise their internal norms, but they do not have to. Members of the club or employees of a company could then determine the meaning, purpose and wording of the affected norm on the pin board of the profile.

Clubs and companies see in the Law Directory the rules imposed on them by the State through its legislation for their administration. The links to the appropriate laws and paragraphs are displayed automatically. To do this, an algorithm accesses the statutes or General Terms and Conditions and the records of the club in the Club Directory[29] and of the company in the Labour Directory[30] .

Citizens can create their own habit profiles, which can be joined by any number of users to share experiences and passions on the habit profile pinboard.

---

29 Ministry of Family Affairs - 9.6.1 Club Directory
30 Ministry of Labour - 13 Labour Directory

4.7.3 Groups

Ministries each form a group in which they group all the norms they have adopted. Clubs do the same for their statutes and companies for their general terms and conditions.

The various codes are organised into groups. This allows ministries, their parties and citizens to order the existing laws in a way that is comprehensible, understandable and thus lawful for them. A new code is a new group, a set of similar codes is a group with subgroups.

4.7.4 Formulation of improvements

Citizens can participate as users with their profile from the Persons Directory on the noticeboards of profiles and groups in order to formulate improvements in this forum. To test a norm for its future developments, the programme "Policy Manager"[31] can be played.

All citizens entitled to view norms can read, comment on and rate them at any time. If the rating is overwhelmingly negative, the politicians who were responsible for the decision on the norm can decide whether to change the norm in voting with those affected.

In the case of state norms, a negative rating is connected with the question of whether one also wants to contribute one's vote to the associated repeal quorum. If a repeal quorum of 60% of the affected citizens is reached, the state norm is resubmitted to the legislative process of the ministries involved. If the ministers do not take care of this matter, their deselection quorum will increase. However, if the ministers do not take care of the matter within at least 18 months, a committee is automatically opened so that the norm can be publicly negotiated and abolished or amended by voting.

Through the comment function, the modulator[32] can be used to reformulate state norms directly online and to win majorities for a certain formulation. The responsible minister can adopt or amend this wording so that his deselection

---

31 Ministry of Digital Affairs - 15.5 Policy Manager
32 Ministry of Digital Affairs - 14.5 Modulator

quorum does not increase.

4.8 Areas of law[33]

All areas of law are there to guarantee human rights, to impose duties on persons and to distribute responsibility for persons fairly. All areas of law can be used by different political levels to distribute and regularise responsibilities and rules. Constitutional law is supreme and breaks international, national and municipal law that contradicts it. National law breaks international and municipal law that conflicts with it. Municipal law can break national and international law within the territory of the municipality if the people and affected citizens of the municipality agree to it in a subsidiarity vote[34] . Police and courts review compliance with the different rules in different regions in their rulings. The constitution, laws and international law are decisive in the review.

Civil law, criminal law, state law and constitutional law are the applicable areas of law. Citizens are considered persons who act in a civil and criminal law role, for example, as a neighbour, spouse, consumer, employee or entrepreneur. The state, which includes all politicians and state employees in state institutions and their work instructions in the form of laws and regulations, administrative instructions or service instructions. Persons in the state service can commit legal offences in state and constitutional law in addition to civil and criminal law. All areas of law have a 20-year statute of limitations. Exceptions are constitutional law and criminal law for offences of killing and rape of minors, where there is no statute of limitations.

Suspected violations of any of the areas of law can be reported by citizens to any police station. Complaints against state agencies can also be made to the Public Prosecutor's Office, the Federal Moderator's Office[35] and Surveillance Television[36] ,

33 §7 Personal rights: KV Art.8, §133 Precedence of and compliance with national law: BV Art.49, §249,7,8 Criminal law, §119 Governing law: BV Art.190
34 Ministry of State Organisation - 10.3 Subsidiarity vote
35 Ministry of State Organisation - 4.4.2 External Service
36 Ministry of Media - 12 Surveillance Television

which must initiate a preliminary investigation.

4.8.1 Civil law[37]

In civil law proceedings, citizens take each other to court. The place of jurisdiction is the defendant's place of residence. The reason for these proceedings is that citizens accuse each other of unjust acts, which are usually based on treaties between the two parties. The Ministry of Justice is responsible for legislation in the individual areas of civil law, namely the law of persons, property law, law of obligations, tort law, family law, inheritance law,[38] equal treatment law and civil procedure law[39] . In civil law, labour court proceedings are also conducted and when companies are accused by citizens or other entrepreneurs.

4.8.2 Criminal law[40]

In criminal proceedings, the state takes citizens to court. The reason for these proceedings is that citizens have violated democratically enacted laws that are enshrined in the domestic codes. The Ministry of Justice legislates on substantive criminal law[41] and criminal procedure law[42] . The ministries, for their part, can enact criminal laws and thus form the ancillary criminal law.

The criminal justice procedure provides for preliminary investigations and, if necessary, coercive measures at the beginning, which may also include deprivation of liberty. This is followed by judicial proceedings and, if necessary, punitive measures, which may also include deprivation of liberty.

Deprivation of liberty must always be ordered by a judge. In case of imminent danger, police officers may detain persons for up to 24 hours until a judge orders pre-trial detention.

37 §248,1 Civil law: BV Art. 122, §30,2 Judicial proceedings: BV Art.30
38 http://www.gesetze-im-internet.de/bgb/
39 http://www.gesetze-im-internet.de/zpo/
40 §32,4,6 Deprivation of liberty: BV Art.31, KV Art.25, §249,1
Criminal law: BV Art. 123, §250 Victim assistance: BV Art. 124
41 https://www.gesetze-im-internet.de/stgb/
42 https://www.gesetze-im-internet.de/stpo/

Damage incurred in criminal prosecution is compensated for all those persons who have been wrongly caught up in criminal prosecution proceedings and have suffered material damage or deprivation of liberty. Victims and witnesses are protected in the best possible way in criminal proceedings. Victims whose physical, psychological or sexual integrity has been impaired are entitled to psychological care and rehabilitation measures as well as the best possible medical care. All victims are entitled to financial compensation, which is to be paid by the offenders in the So-called offender-victim settlement. If offenders are unable to make the payment, the Ministry of Justice makes the payment and lets the offender work off the amount in detention. The imprisonment is extended accordingly. State assistance for victims of crime or their survivors is offered by the Social Villages.

4.8.3 State law[43]

In state law proceedings, citizens take the state to court. The reason for these proceedings is that the state withholds rights or duties from citizens or distributes them unequally. All state services are based on the norms of the ministries, which form state law. The Ministry of Justice issues the procedures in the State Procedure Law when persons take the state to court. The Remit Courts are the first instance, the National Court of Justice the second instance and the Constitutional Court the third instance.

4.8.4 Constitutional law

In constitutional proceedings, the people take the state to court. The reason for these proceedings is that the state has enacted norms that are not in accordance with the constitution. Constitutional law is founded only on the constitution.

43§247,2,3 State law

5 Court proceedings[44]

All court proceedings follow uniform principles. Plaintiff and defendant are the two parties in court proceedings. Judges and judicial officers provide them with a legal hearing by taking note of their CVs and statements on the facts of the case under trial and hearing them in court proceedings in order to be able to pronounce a reasoned judgement. These procedures are the same for all cases and ensure fair treatment by applying the law in the shortest possible procedural time. Court judgments must establish a chain of reasoning in the written reasons between the case, the judgment and the law affected.

Defendants have a right to know promptly what charges they are facing and to defend themselves against them or have them defended by legal counsel. Plaintiffs and defendants, as well as their counsel, have a right to access the records pertaining to the court proceedings and to be advised of the remedies available to them if they are dissatisfied with the judgment.

Only when no more appeals are filed are court proceedings considered concluded. Only from this point on do judgments become legally binding. Until that time, the presumption of innocence applies. This means that due to a lack of evidence and persistent doubt, the defendant is presumed innocent and must be acquitted.

During court hearings, the plaintiff, defendant and court staff as well as visitors do not have to be present together in one courtroom. Statements can be transmitted between different court locations via video and intranet. Travel times and travel costs are thus saved. The arbitration proceedings are only held digitally. All other court proceedings take place in a real courtroom. Several courtrooms become necessary when video transmissions are used. Lay judges can be connected to the courtroom via video telephony using their People's Computers.

If expert opinions are obtained in court proceedings that may result in defendants having to remain in detention for the rest

---

44§29,1,2 General procedural guarantees: BV Art.29, §30,3,4,5 Judicial proceedings: BV Art.30, KV Art.26, §32,3,5b Deprivation of liberty: BV Art.31, KV Art.25, §33 Criminal proceedings: BV Art.32, §249,6 Criminal law: BV Art. 123a, §125,1,6 Judicial authorities

of their lives, then these expert opinions must be prepared by three independent assessors who are experienced professionals and who have been able to talk to the defendant in person and see all the evidence.

5.1 Legal process

If the plaintiff or defendant is dissatisfied with the judgement, they can appeal to the next higher court until the legal process is exhausted. The legal process consists of several instances. After the court proceedings in the first instance, an appeal can be filed. This means that the same case is newly heard by other judges and, if necessary, other lawyers, with new evidence being taken. On appeal, the laws are considered just, but their application is considered presumptively unjust. If the plaintiff or defendant considers the judgement to be unjust because the applicable laws only allow such unjust judgements, a revision can be filed by which a change of the laws can be obtained. Appeals and revisions may be lodged within 2 months of the pronouncement of the judgement. In the case of constitutional complaints based on a revision or a petition for a review of norms, the Constitutional Court is the last or only instance.

Courts differ depending on the instance in which court proceedings are located. While Municipal Courts are the receiving body for cases, Remit Courts are responsible for appeal cases and the National Court of Justice for revision cases. On appeal, a case is re-examined by other judges and on revision, the interpretation of the laws is newly made. In revision, faults or weaknesses in the law can be discovered, forcing the legislature to change it. In the revision, it is also possible that a law in its interpretation violates or would violate the constitution in an individual case. In this situation, the Constitutional Court is the last judicial instance to issue orders to the legislature.

5.2 Public hearings

Court hearings are generally open to the public, filmed and saved as a video file in the Court Directory in the profile of the case. In the case of minors, visitors, apart from the legal guardians, are excluded and their faces and votes are anonymised in the video recordings. Anonymisation of the face and vote can also be requested by plaintiffs or defendants. If company secrets come to light in a court hearing, the responsible judge may exclude the public in this part and only the court staff and the secrecy holders present may become aware of it.

Public court hearings are not there to put offenders or victims on display, but to review the lawful application of norms in individual cases by directly elected judges.

5.3 Remand

Police authorities may immediately take a person into police custody if there is evidence that he or she has committed a serious criminal offence. A serious offence is any offence in which physical force has been used. Within 24 hours, an offender must be brought before the magistrate at the Municipal Court. This is where the decision is made as to whether pre-trial detention will be issued by a judge via an arrest warrant, which is executed immediately in the courtroom. Pre-trial detention is always used if there is a risk of flight or a risk of repetition.

If the defendant is a flight risk in the ongoing court proceedings, the responsible judge can order pre-trial detention. The pre-trial detention can be suspended by depositing a sum of money as bail, if the judge does not exclude it. The amount of the sum of money is determined by the judge and measured against the amount of directly available assets of the defendant. In order to justify pre-trial detention, the defendant may request a pre-trial hearing. In the event of a judgement against the defendant, he must bear the costs of the pre-trial proceedings himself. Otherwise, the same provisions apply to pre-trial detention as to detention.

For as long as the investigation lasts, the alleged offender must work in prisons where jobs are performed without a long learning period. If an offender is wanted by arrest warrant, detention in pre-trial detention takes place immediately after arrest. Pre-trial detention may last a maximum of 3 months per instance.

After the verdict establishes the seriousness of the guilt in the court proceedings, the prisoner is transferred to a prison that meets his security requirements with a suitable staffing ratio.

5.4 Courts[45]

Court constitutional law regulates the functioning and tasks of the courts. Courts are basically responsible for mediating between disputing parties and settling the dispute. For this purpose, courts make use of the laws that the legislature has provided for this purpose and enforce international, national or municipal law. Courts are independent of any influence and are only dependent on the norms that the majority of the population has agreed to. The Ministry of Justice regulates below which courts are created and for which areas of law they are responsible. All courts are responsible for all areas of law except the Constitutional Court, which is responsible only for constitutional law.

All courts are divided into chambers. A chamber represents the area of accountability of a ministry. As soon as several areas of law are involved in a case, a corresponding number of judges from different chambers preside and form a team. If lay judges are involved in a case, they form a team with the judges.

5.4.1 Court centres

The courts are set up in court centres. There are courtrooms, consultation rooms and offices. All courtrooms have a sound system with table microphones and speakers on the ceiling, a 360° 3D camera, a beamer on the ceiling and a partially

---

45§30,1 Judicial proceedings: BV Art.30, §247,4 State law: BV Art.173, §123 Courts: KV Art.97

transparent screen that can be lowered from the ceiling of the room in the middle, directly in front of the witness chair. At the front sit the lay judges and centrally the judges. On the left sit the defendants with their lawyers, on the right the prosecution or the plaintiffs with their lawyers. In the centre of the room sit the witnesses, face to face with the judges and lay judges. Behind the witnesses sits the audience. There are three entrances and exits to this room. Centrally at the back for the audience, on the left for the lawyers, plaintiffs and defendants, and centrally at the front for the judges and lay judges into a deliberation room with its own exit.

Through the 360° 3D camera and microphones, all public sessions in the Court Directory are archived after the negotiation and made available to users on the intranet. Courts keep the statistics of the administration of justice in the Court Directory, which can be viewed by all intranet users. There is at least one courtroom in each court centre equipped with 4 cameras to broadcast court hearings in real time on state television and in the Court Directory. Through the construction and operation of court centres, every court hearing can be held in every room in order to permanently utilise the available space.

5.4.2 Arbitration Court

The Arbitration Court is an offer before the first instance, i.e. the Municipal Courts. The Arbitration Court offers a voluntary procedure of arbitration for out-of-court conflict resolution. Proceedings with a value in dispute of less than 1000 Dollars must first be heard by the Arbitration Court.

It is accessible via the Court Directory and has software that allows lay judges to access services from the Algoracle[46] to simulate the case and the law. Plaintiffs and defendants are asked to provide information about the case via their People's Computer. With this interactive form, the information on the case is provided by keyword entry. For each keyword, further questions are asked, which are ticked off. For example, entering the keyword "neighbourhood dispute" would have

46Ministry of Digital Affairs - 15.3 Algoracle

the selection of "rent, property, noise" to choose from. Using the case data, laws are displayed that are proposed for the regularisation of the case. Plaintiffs and defendants now sort out laws they think are inappropriate or add others and can mark certain passages they think are apt. The laws are automatically listed by the algorithm divided into pros and cons. There are always incriminating and approving laws in a case, which is represented by this.

Furthermore, a verbatim description of the case must be recorded, by text, sound, image or video. If contradictions are automatically detected, the programme asks the plaintiff or defendant to provide further information. Untypical situations are rated personally by the lay judges or, in the case of difficult questions, a judge can be consulted. These case descriptions of the plaintiffs and defendants as well as the automatically found laws and the passages of law marked by the plaintiffs and defendants serve as a basis for the lay judges' decisions.

The lay judges in the Arbitration Court are selected in the same way and perform the same work as all other lay judges, only without a judge. They receive a lump-sum expense allowance for their work per case and amount in dispute. In arbitration proceedings, both parties bear the costs for the lay judges jointly.

The lay judges in the Arbitration Court will never see themselves and the claimants and respondents in person in a negotiation of the case. The entire procedure is intranet-based and time-limited. Once a plaintiff opens a case, the defendant must respond within a time limit. The lay judges then form their verdict and vote until a 90% majority of the lay judges vote in favour of a verdict. Against this verdict, ordinary court proceedings can be opened in the Municipal Court.

5.4.3 Municipal Courts[47]

Municipal Courts are the first instance for civil law, criminal law or state law proceedings. Constitutional law proceedings can be referred to the Constitutional Court via the Municipal

---

47 §248,2 Civil law: BV Art. 122, §249,2 Criminal law: BV Art. 123, §125,2 Judicial instances, §122 Municipal Courts: BV Art.191b

Court. Every municipality, or in the case of low capacity, a group of municipalities, has a Municipal Court. All citizens of the municipality or group of municipalities elect the judges in a direct election of persons and provide them with a deselection quorum.

If the necessary expertise is lacking at one court location, judges and public prosecutors from the other courts are lent out temporarily or integrated at short notice via the intranet. The Municipal Court located in the catchment area of the defendant's place of residence has the responsibility.

If, according to the defendant, the plaintiff or the public prosecutor's office, not all facts are taken into account in the verdict of the municipal court proceedings, one can appeal. The case will now be newly heard in the appropriate Remit Court, possibly with new evidence and witnesses, but compulsorily by different judges than those of the first instance.

5.4.4 Remit Courts[48]

Remit Courts are the second instance and newly hear cases on appeal from the Municipal Courts. A Remit Court always has only one chamber, i.e. it deals with only one area of law of a ministry. Accordingly, there are 18 Remit Courts, which are located in the capital cities of the respective ministries. If the workload is too high, Remit Courts can open branches. Judges and lay judges are involved in all negotiations of the Remit Courts. Judges are elected by the people in a direct election of persons, with a deselection quorum.

If, according to the defendant, the plaintiff or the prosecution, not all laws are correctly interpreted in a judgement, one can lodge a revision. The laws from the previous case and, if necessary, other or new laws, are applied to the case in the National Court of Justice.

48§125,3 Judicial instances, §121 Remit Courts: BV Art.191a

5.4.5 National Court of Justice[49]

The National Court of Justice is the third instance and thus the final instance for cases of civil, criminal and state law. Revision cases are heard here. The National Court of Justice is the highest court for the state.

A threshold can be set for cases as long as not many persons are affected. Thus, cases below this amount in dispute cannot be brought in revision. Cases whose legal position is clear and the complaint behind the revision is therefore unfounded are judged in summary proceedings within one session.

The National Court of Justice is divided into civil law, criminal law and state law chambers. If the National Court of Justice finds that a law is unconstitutional, it must refer the case to the Constitutional Court. State law cases also include disputes between state agencies, namely between ministries, between the national, international and municipal levels or between municipalities.

The Public Prosecutor's Office of the National Court of Justice can refer cases of national importance. National importance is always given when politicians have violated laws or the constitution in office. Such cases are dealt with in a committee of enquiry[50] and in court proceedings. The committee of enquiry is considered to be the conclusion of the taking of evidence.

All negotiations before the National Court of Justice involve lay judges who have been lay judges at least 3 times before. The judges are elected by the people in a direct election of persons and have a deselection quorum. What is special about the Court is that it administers itself, because it also judges laws passed by the Ministry of Justice. The leader is himself a judge of the Court and is directly elected by the judges of the Court and re-elected if at least 50% of the judges are dissatisfied with his conduct of office and express a vote of no confidence in him.

49§125.4 Judicial instances, §116 Position of the National Court of Justice: BV Art.188, §117 Responsibilities of the National Court of Justice: BV Art.189, §118 Admission to the National Court of Justice: BV Art.191

50Ministry of State Organisation - 12.5.2 Committee of enquiry

5.4.5.1 International affairs

The National Court of Justice judges disputes between states on the basis of international law and consults with the court of the other affected state to reach a decision. Judgments can be uniform, but do not have to be. The National Court of Justice is the sole instance for domestic or inter-state disputes in state law proceedings without direct citizen participation.

If, in the course of communitarisation, the Ministry of Justice is absorbed into an International Union[51] , the National Court of Justice becomes part of the new International Court of Justice. Once communitarisation into a federal state is complete, the National Court of Justice is dissolved and the International Court of Justice becomes the new National Court of Justice.

5.4.5.2 Committee of enquiry[52]

As soon as a case of damage has been facilitated or caused by state failure, a committee of enquiry is established after a report has been made to the police. The Ministry of State Organisation determines who can convene a committee of enquiry, when and how.[53]

Committees of enquiry are organised and moderated by the Surveillance Television.[54] They are public meetings, like any other committee. However, here a court hearing is first held by the National Court of Justice to take evidence and prepare the charge sheet, followed by a legislative process to remove the causes.

In the first part, witnesses, assessors and investigators are heard, evidence is sifted through, justifications are sought and an indictment is formulated. The audience consists of party members of the different party wings and affected citizens. The panel consists of the responsible politicians as well as judges of the specialist department from the Remit Courts and the National Court of Justice. At times, the panel also includes

51 Ministry of Foreign Affairs - 5.8 International Union
52 §97 Investigation Committee: BV Art.153
53 Ministry of State Organisation - 12.5.2 Committee of enquiry
54 Ministry of Media Affairs - 12.3.4.1 Committee of enquiry

various experts as assessors. These are responsible ministers to explain the ministry's working methods, as well as scientists who examine the psyche and socialisation of the offender and victim to illustrate motives. State employees of the accused politicians and investigators from the Surveillance Television's responsible monitoring team[55] are called as witnesses.

Citizens can propose and rate who will be called as a witness and what questions they will be asked on the Committee of Enquiry's profile page in the Committee Directory. During the committee, further interim questions can be asked. For the purpose of taking evidence, the committee of enquiry is entitled to information rights vis-à-vis the politicians and their state employees, as well as the right to inspect all files relating to the case and investigative powers for searches and undercover investigations. Searches and undercover investigations are conducted by the Surveillance Television monitoring team.

Once it is clear who is responsible for an offence, the Public Prosecutor's Office of the National Court of Justice brings charges and holds the state employees liable to official liability if they have violated the constitution or certain laws. The court proceedings continue with the indictment drawn up and a verdict found. However, this continuation takes place in a courtroom of the National Court of Justice.

The second part in the committee of enquiry is taken over by the Ministry of State Organisation[56] . There, it is a matter of eliminating the damage and causes as well as formulating the necessary norms, which are put to a vote of the affected citizens.

5.4.6 Constitutional Court[57]

The Constitutional Court is the fourth instance after the third instance has established the responsibility of the Constitutional Court in the revision. If unconstitutional laws would lead to a miscarriage of justice, the Constitutional Court can, after a revision case, annul the force of the law in this case and

---

55 Ministry of Media Affairs - 12.1 Monitoring team
56 Ministry of State Organisation - 12.5.2.2 Solution finding
57 §125,5,7 Judicial instances, §120 Constitutional Court: BV Art.191a

force the legislature to revise the unconstitutional law within a period of time. The Constitutional Court is the supreme court for the citizens.

Citizens and ministries can report laws for unconstitutionality in standard control proceedings and thus file a constitutional complaint. The Constitutional Court is the first instance for this. Norm control procedures require a lead time of 6 months, during which the laws under review are to be discussed and rated on the homepage of the Law Directory. After this period, either the responsible minister has acted or a People's Committee has been convened. If this is not the case, the Constitutional Court examines whether the law is unconstitutional. If so, the responsible minister must, within a time limit, amend the law, abolish it or have it negotiated by a People's Committee and voted on by referendum. If the constitution needs to be amended, the case must be so moving that a revision quorum is triggered and a constitutional committee convened. The Constitutional Committee is the final authority and is able to amend constitutional articles and laws affected in the case simultaneously.

The judges of the Constitutional Court are elected by the people in a direct election of persons and have a deselection quorum. If the judges of the Constitutional Court lack expertise, they can call in more expert judges from the Remit Courts for a case consultation or court hearing. There are no lay judges in the Constitutional Court.

5.5 Court Directory

Every case that is heard in court is given a profile. In the profile are all police investigations from the Investigation Directory and all pleadings of the lawyers. A programme translates the contents into a virtual simulation in which missing and contradictory statements by the plaintiffs and defendants are displayed.

Each court is a group in which all the judges, lawyers and public prosecutors who reside there are members. They are divided into sub-groups in areas of accountability. Court hearings that affect the whole people or are of special public interest are broadcast on Government Television[58]. All public negotiations are video-streamed on the intranet in the Court Directory. All court hearings are stored in the Court Directory. The Court Directory is the central input screen for all cases that are and have been heard in domestic courts. In this way, all paper-based filing systems are to be digitised. All entry screens contain areas with personal data that are only visible to state employees and the affected defendants or plaintiffs. The other areas are the course of events, the application of the paragraphs and the judgement including the reasons. The paragraphs are linked to the Law Directory.

5.5.1 Rate judgments

In each case profile, there is an overview of affected laws and all previous judicially adjudicated cases in which the same laws were applied and how the verdict is formulated. The judgements are anonymised, but it should become clear before which judge, in which court, at which time a case was heard. At this point, judgements can be judged as "just", "wrongful", "too lenient" or "too harsh". Users also have the option of rating individual passages and the entire text of the judgement. By linking to the judge's profile in the Labour Directory, users can vote for the deselection quorum. In order to consolidate one's wish to be voted out of office, it is possible to view all judgements of a judge via the Court Directory. Before deselection, the user is asked to view an overview of the judge's judgements over the past two years, which are listed in tabular form and can be displayed as a graph in the monthly history. An algorithm calculates the severity of a judge in two steps.

First, the case is tried virtually to create a default value. For this purpose, the paragraphs used are taken and a range is opened between the minimum and maximum sentence that has been set in the law. Furthermore, the amount of damage that the defendant and the plaintiff have stated is included. To calculate the external circumstances of the plaintiff and the defendant, the algorithm uses the data from all the

---

58 Ministry of Media - 7 Government Television

directories in order to be able to include the living situation. The Ministry of Justice staff enters keywords, numbers and degrees of hardship for all life situations. In the case of income or illness, a scale can easily be created. With feelings of fear or guilt, it looks different. For this, the ministry staff is assisted by teachers from the Ministry of Education. The elaborated rating catalogue has to be submitted to the people for rating, as well as any changes. Furthermore, the algorithm takes into account all past comparable cases in the rating.

Secondly, the judge's severity is calculated and given as a second value. It is calculated from the lawful sentence, the fixed amount of damage as well as information from the judge to take into account the external circumstances.

5.6 Court staff[59]

Court staff administer justice in court proceedings and provide advice to plaintiffs or defendants as legal counsel. If a defendant is deprived of liberty, he or she must be provided with legal counsel. Court staff are subject to the professional code of conduct for lawyers, patent attorneys and judges as prescribed by the Ministry of Justice below.

The training of court staff takes place through the nationally standardised law degree programme with at least one minor subject. In law studies, all areas of law, the corresponding legal texts and court proceedings are discussed and judgements are analysed and decided in examinations themselves. All courses of study that fit into one of the 18 ministries are available for election as a minor subject. The Ministry of Justice examines all courses of study together with the subject areas of the colleges to see whether the content taught there covers the area of a ministry.

Each ministry has its area of accountability for a remit and acts by virtue of the constitution, law and regulation to fulfil a purpose committed to the welfare of the people. Court staff must know these sources in order to be able to argue and judge professionally. While all the remits of the ministries are

---

59 §29,3 General procedural guarantees: BV Art.29, §32,5a Deprivation of liberty: KV Art.25

still represented in the Municipal Court, the Remit Courts only hear cases that cover the legal domain of a ministry.

For example, in a dispute between tenant and landlord, this would be the Ministry of Economy of the economic form in which the lease was concluded. In this example, it would be a civil case conducted at the Remit Court without a prosecution because it is an appeal case.

In the National Court of Justice, there is a public prosecutor's office that defends the law passed by that ministry. Thus, the field of law always extends to the area of accountability of a ministry. If several ministries are affected, specialised staff of judges and prosecutors with a suitable minor must be lent out by the respective chamber. Particularly in the Remit Courts, it is necessary for the legal staff to develop in-depth professional judgement. Judges, lay judges and public prosecutors must be nationals.

5.6.1 Judge[60]

Judges are impartial. This means that they do not favour either plaintiffs or defendants and treat them impartially and without prejudice. Impartial does not mean that judges may not favour policies of one party wing. On the contrary, this is desirable and part of the election programme of a judge in the election of persons process. Judges are independent. This means that they are not dependent or biased in any way on the side of either the plaintiffs or the defendants. Judges are only dependent on the will of those entitled to vote, who are able to elect and deselect judges.

5.6.1.1 Necessary qualifications

In order to stand for election as a judge, one must have successfully completed law studies with a matching minor subject and also be a member of the party that matches the minor subject. Judges are therefore members of at least two

---

60 §31,1 Legal protection: KV Art.26, §124 Judicial independence: BV Art.191c

parties.

For example, that would be law and political science if you are in the justice and state organisation party. As a judge, one could then be appointed in cases that have to do with state organisation. At the Remit Court, one would then judge in the State Organisation Court, at the National Court of Justice in the State Law Chamber and in the Constitutional Court as a State Organisation Judge.

It is possible to extend the specialist department to more remits. For this, the corresponding party membership and the extra-occupational study of another corresponding minor subject at a college is necessary.

In order to stand for election to a particular instance, at least three years of service at the previous instance are considered a prerequisite, which does not apply to Municipal Courts. This makes it possible, for example, for thirty-year-olds to sit on the Constitutional Court. Despite the necessary years of service, a balanced age distribution in all instances is important in order to adequately represent the generations in the country.

5.6.1.2 Eligibility

Everyone who wants to become a judge stands for election. Every judge knows when colleagues are retiring and the latest time to apply for their posts. Vacancies or new elections for a post are publicly advertised so that the judicial party can compile the list of candidates from all those interested. Those who wish to apply for more than one post must assign a rank to each post as to how much they would like that post. Those entitled to vote then decide for which post they would like the judge. Whichever judge receives the majority of votes for a post is considered elected. Each voter can cast one vote for each post to be filled. One can therefore vote for a candidate more than once for all the posts for which he has applied. In the event of a tie in popularity for several posts, the candidate may choose one of these posts himself. In that case, the runners-up for the other posts move up. Normally, several judges do not retire at the same time, so that one post has to be filled, which makes the election process similar to the usual election of persons process.[61]

5.6.1.3 Voting rights

Judges are elected on a municipal or national basis. Accordingly, citizens of a municipality or the people are entitled to vote. Judges are members of the Ministry of Justice party from the time they are nominated for election until the end of their term. Judges are directly elected and dismissed by deselection quorum. Their profile pages can be found in the Labour Directory, where you can put your cross for the deselection quorum if you are dissatisfied with the judgements of that judge.

Elections for Municipal Court judges are held in the catchment area of the associated town hall. All citizens living in the catchment area of the town hall are eligible to vote.

Elections for judges of Remit Courts, the National Court of Justice and the Constitutional Court are held throughout the country. In the election campaign, candidates are supported by the two parties of which they are members. Each candidate should be able to express his or her position. Broadcasters of the Ministry of Media Affairs and the digital service of the Ministry of Digital Affairs help in this. Airtime and advertising material of the intranet are provided free of charge.

5.6.2 Lay judges

By having the population act as lay judges, the moral judgement of the people is strengthened. Lay judges are nationals of age of majority with certain qualifications that are useful in the case. Lay judges are not used in the first instance, but only before the first instance in the Arbitration Court. In the second and third instance, lay judges are a popular voice, similar to that of a judge. They are similar persons to jurors on a jury, because each lay judge represents a question of conscience. Thus, the jurists among the lay judges are pragmatic, the lay judges with similarities to the accused and defendants are emotional,

---

61 Ministry of State Organisation - 9.9 Elections of persons

and the age and gender mates reflect the socialisation of the generation.

In the Arbitration Court, lay judges judge a case as a team, without a judge. In the second and third instance, lay judges work with the judge on the verdict. The judge, however, has the right to incorporate more or less of this into the judgement. The number of lay judges per case is determined on the basis of the amount in dispute. Up to 100,000 Dollars there are 10 lay judges, after that 2 more lay judges for each additional 100,000 Dollars. The lay judges incur additional court costs for the loser of the case. The lay judges are paid at the minimum wage and are considered to be reimbursed for their honorary service. The lay judges can live all over the country and participate digitally via their People's Computer or live near the court and participate in real life.

5.6.2.1 Selection

Lay judges with suitable qualifications are found by an algorithm by retrieving data from the Persons Directory, Education Directory and Labour Directory. The lay judges are randomly selected from all eligible persons. If one is selected, one may refuse a maximum of 3 times. If one accepts the selection, one may refuse again for the next 3 requests and so on.

The qualifications for a case are distributed as a percentage of the total number of lay judges appointed for a case. 20% of the lay judges must have completed legal training, graduated from or recognised by a state college. 20% of the lay judges should have personal similarities with the plaintiff, 20% with the defendant, 20% should have professional expertise through training or work experience, and 10% are of the same age and gender as the plaintiff and 10% as the defendant. The data comes from all profiles of all directories of a lay judge. The lay judges themselves know which category they belong to and the other lay judges and responsible judges know that too, no one else. The entire team of lay judges receives an overview of all lay judges involved at the beginning.

Personal bindings with the plaintiffs, defendants and among

the lay judges are deliberately excluded. If a selected lay judge knows plaintiffs or defendants, he must report this and plaintiffs or defendants must confirm it. Then the lay judge is replaced.

5.6.2.2 Teamwork

The judge and lay judge cooperate with each other in court proceedings. First, all lay judges and the judge meet in a real or virtual place. There, the judge informs the lay judges about their task and the case, and the lay judges can ask questions. The indictment makes it clear which laws are supposed to have been violated here. The court hearing follows, in which lay judges and magistrates separately examine the case, question witnesses, sift through the evidence presented, in order to negotiate the guilt and sentence in sessions away from the court hearing. As soon as guilt and sentence have been found, the judge and lay judge meet again. There they present their decisions for guilt and sentence, question and discuss the decisions and agree on a common interpretation.

Since the judge is directly elected by the people, he always has a veto right. If the lay judges feel that they have not been given sufficient consideration, they can enter this in the Court Directory in the profile of the case. These entries are to be regarded as vetoes by a judge because he has deliberately ignored the lay judges. The more vetoes a judge collects in the course of his career, the higher the risk of reaching the deselection quorum.

5.6.3 Public prosecutor's office[62]

Prosecutors represent the people in prosecuting persons who have violated laws and constitutional articles. Injured citizens can act as joint plaintiffs. Only in civil cases are they not involved. Citizens can report misconduct caused by state agencies to the Public Prosecutor's Office. Prosecutorial

---

62 §70,2,3 Supervision: BV Art.169, §71,4 Review of effectiveness: BV Art.170

personnel are recruited from the top 30% of law school graduates at state colleges. Successful lawyers can also be recruited.

The public prosecutor's office is part of the superintendence of tasks of the state. In addition to their work in court, their prosecutors are also part of the Surveillance Television monitoring teams. Public prosecutors cannot be held to any secrecy obligations in their investigations. They treat company or private secrets confidentially and are subject to secrecy away from the courtroom, i.e. they are not allowed to disclose company or private secrets to third parties.

The Ministry of Justice is supplied with cases by the Ministry of Security when the security agencies investigate offenders or suspects. The prosecutors work closely with the security forces and have authority over them. For the prosecution of criminals by the police, clear rules are laid down in the police law as to which investigations by the security agencies must be ordered by a judge or a public prosecutor before they can be lawfully carried out.

5.6.3.1 Charges against security agencies[63]

Charges against security agencies must be filed with the responsible public prosecutor's office. The public prosecutor's office responsible is always the one in whose vicinity the reported security agencies are deployed. The report itself is accepted by every domestic public prosecutor's office and forwarded to the appropriate office. For each complaint against security agencies, a case is opened in the Court Directory so that citizens can see whether the complaint has actually been filed and how it is being handled. The Public Prosecutor's Office is obliged to investigate arbitrary acts by state employees, secure evidence and, if there is sufficient evidence, open arbitrary rule proceedings in the appropriate Remit Court. The proceedings can be transferred to a committee of enquiry for the responsible politician by a 30% veto quorum of those entitled to vote.

---

63 §3,2,3 Protection against state arbitrariness: BV Art.9

5.6.4 Lawyers

Lawyers can organise themselves as freelancers or in law firms and open a company in an economic form of their choice. In law school, the minor subjects in which one wants to further one's education determine the specialist departments in order to be admitted to a certain chamber with which one may represent such cases as a lawyer. It is always possible for lawyers to handle more or fewer areas of law, provided they have completed the necessary training in the areas of law. Lawyers are not required to be members of the Judicial Party or the party of their minor subject unless they wish to stand for election to judicial office.

5.7 Financing[64]

In any court proceedings, the Ministry of Justice advances the legal fees and court costs. The legal fees and court costs are paid by the loser of the case. If the case is won, the winners do not have to pay any legal fees. After the conclusion of the proceedings, the loser must pay back to the state all costs for all instances and lawyers called upon. If necessary, he must take out a loan or work off the outstanding amount in detention. Persons and companies can insure themselves against the court costs and lawyers' fees, but not against the sentence.

5.7.1 Criminal and constitutional law

The administration of justice in criminal and constitutional law is financed through value added tax. The fewer crimes citizens commit and the better citizens, state employees and norms align with the constitution, the fewer court proceedings need to be conducted and the lower the value added tax. If the value added tax increases, all laws must be listed according to their frequency used in court proceedings before the budget vote. Laws with a high frequency are accordingly reviewed by citizens and can be changed or deleted by those entitled to vote through the repeal quorum. Politicians are encouraged

---

64 §31 Legal protection: KV Art.26

to change policies in such a way that fewer violations of the affected laws occur in order to preserve their deselection quorum.

5.7.2 Civil and state law

For civil and state law, there is legal expenses insurance or the private hiring of lawyers. Those who cannot afford a lawyer here can defend themselves in the first instance and receive a public defender from the second instance onwards. Those who lose a case bear the costs of the proceedings and, if necessary, have to work them off in detention.

5.7.3 Commercial legal protection

The law on fees in the field of industrial property protection differs from the law on fees in the field of private law legal protection as follows. Entrepreneurs who have to pursue court proceedings for their companies only receive legal services if they can pay for them. Entrepreneurs in the Planned Economy and Social Market Economy are compulsorily insured with their companies in the state legal protection insurance and accordingly receive legal care within the scope of the insurance benefits. The Free Market Economy maintains its own legal expenses insurance, in which citizens and companies can insure themselves.

5.7.4 Hopeless legal challenges

Legal petitions that appear futile must violate several laws and constitutional articles. These legal petitions concern all areas of law and can only be resolved in court if the plaintiffs deposit a sufficient amount with the responsible court cashier before the proceedings begin. The amount must be sufficient to pay the costs of the proceedings if the plaintiffs lose the court proceedings. The deposit must be made newly for each instance. If they win the case, the treasury must pay the costs of the proceedings and amend the necessary laws and constitutional articles. If the case is so convincing that injustice is being perpetuated by the existing laws and constitutional articles, a majority of the people will be found to change the norms affected. In the event of success, the plaintiffs will receive all their deposited amounts back.

5.7.5 Court costs

The court costs consist of the costs for the buildings and the staff of the courts, including the judges' salaries. Judges' pay is itemised in the budget vote and can be changed by the citizens. Court costs may be borne by the Ministry of Justice if the state has been a plaintiff in the proceedings and has lost the court proceedings. Court costs that are not borne by the Ministry of Justice receive a 10% profit mark-up. This profit mark-up first finances the costs to be borne by the Ministry of Justice. Remaining amounts flow into the state treasury. If a loss occurs, it is compensated by tax money and in the following year the court costs have to be increased in such a way that the amount can be repaid.

5.7.6 Lawyer's fee

The Ministry of Justice regulates the law on lawyers' fees in voting with the associations of lawyers and puts it to a vote of the people. Lawyers are remunerated with a flat fee based on the amount in dispute. The fee is made up of a fixed amount and an hourly rate. The fixed amount is determined by a table listing the limits of the amount in dispute and the corresponding amounts.[65] The hourly fee is determined by a table in which the won and lost cases are related to the amount in dispute of these cases in order to calculate a success rate from them. The success rate serves as a multiplier by which the basic amount of the hourly wage is multiplied. The basic amount is 2 times the Social Market Economy minimum wage.
The fixed amounts per limit of dispute and the basic amount of the hourly wage are set by the Ministry of Justice in cooperation

---

65https://www.gesetze-im-internet.de/rvg/anlage_2.html

with the Association of Lawyers. The Association of Lawyers is a group in the Court Directory that has subgroups for areas of law, remits and courts of which only lawyers can be members. Lawyers who run their companies in the Barter Economy or Free Market Economy can contract the fees themselves with their clients. The fees described above can be exceeded or undercut in the process.

5.7.7 Legal expenses insurance[66]

The Ministry of Justice operates a legal expenses insurance scheme that pre-funds all court proceedings so that only losers have to make payments. Losers must reimburse the costs of the proceedings or work them off in detention. The insurance conditions of the state legal expenses insurance are determined democratically by all contributors together with the Ministry of Justice in a committee.
Costs of court proceedings in civil and state law are borne personally by legal expenses insurers or losers.
The state legal protection insurance of the Ministry of Justice offers these insurance services to citizens of the Barter Economy and Free Market Economy for a fee. Citizens and companies who work full-time in the Planned Economy or Social Market Economy pay into the compulsory insurance through business taxes.[67] There are 3 risk classes with 3 contribution levels. The more often one claims legal expenses insurance through one's own fault, the higher the premium and vice versa, similar to the no-claims class for motor vehicle insurance. Business taxes are adjusted accordingly. Companies are entitled to deduct the tax increases due to premium increases from the wages of the originating employees.
Free Market Economy legal expenses insurers can determine their own insurance conditions and make them the basis for all their insurance contracts.

66§31,2-5 Legal protection
67Ministry of Social Market Economy - 17.5.5 Legal expenses insurance

5.8 Assessment of the damage

The task of the courts is to regulate the damage that humans do to each other. The settlement of damages is done firstly by the offenders compensating their victims with a sum of money determined by the court. Secondly, courts set a sentence for wantonly or negligently causing damage in order to prevent such acts in the future.

An offence can cause damage to one or more persons, so-called personal damage. An offence can also cause damage to a community of persons, so-called social damage. Personal and social damage is divided into material and psychological damage. Material damages are things that have been stolen, damaged or destroyed, humans that have been injured or killed, or the environment that has been polluted or damaged. Psychological damage occurs when individuals or communities feel fear or grief after an offence or develop mental illnesses. Material and psychological damage can be repaired by spending sufficient money.

The aim of the court proceedings is firstly to collect sufficient amounts of money through compensation payments from the offenders to compensate the victims. Secondly, the punitive measures should generate sums of money that cover 110% of the costs of the correctional system. If the damage exceeds the life expectancy of the offender, judges must specify a minimum period of imprisonment in their sentences, unless the legislature has specified a time. This minimum duration cannot be reduced by paying for the damage.

5.8.1 Material damage

When someone causes damage and this damage is regulated by a conventional insurance company, this is done via a lump-sum list of benefits from the insurance industry. This list holds, for example, amounts for the value of a car, a house or for a human life. These tables are used to calculate the monetary amount of the material damage. If amounts are unclear, the damage sums are calculated with the help of assessors. The material damage is not measured by the value of the destroyed things, but by the current replacement value of things that are as identical as possible. The estimated costs for material damage represent the costs for restoring the initial condition before the offence. This also includes things that must first be disposed of at a cost before they can be replaced. The aim of court proceedings is to quantify the material damage as precisely as possible in order to determine the amount of compensation to be paid by the offender.

5.8.2 Psychological damage

Damage usually also results in anxiety for the victim and sometimes also for society. Personal psychological damage is measured by costs for therapies and loss of work. The lump sum values are adjusted by the judges to the individual case, taking into account the mental state the victim is in during the court proceedings. For this purpose, the judge may have a private conversation with the victim or commission a psychological assessor.

Costs for psychological therapies alone are not sufficient to also quantify the social psychological damage. In order for the state to give its citizens a sense of security, additional expenditures by affected ministries are often necessary, for example for law enforcement and security agencies, audit services or Youth Welfare Offices. These measures are listed as lump sums in a table for social psychological damage.

This table is established as law by an Ethics Commission[68] of the Ministry of Justice. The Ethics Commission has persons on the panel who have been appointed by the Minister of Justice. These are judges from the various courts, responsible ministers and, where appropriate, ministry staff. Citizens form the audience, among whom offenders and victims can also report. Together, the panel and the audience measure the costs of social psychological damage and link them in a table with corresponding offences. Social psychological damage is graded in the table as lump sums per capita.

---

68 Ministry of State Organisation - 8.5.9 Ethics Commission

Examples of psychological damage:
10$ per day in fear involuntarily suffered by victims
1000$ for assault
2000$ for assault in public
10 000$ for unauthorised entry into a living space
100 000$ for the use of firearms in public

5.8.3 Example robbery

Material damage	Sum in Dollar
Breaking and entering and searching the premises	15 000
Stolen goods	50 000
Damage to road traffic during escape	10 000
Hospital and rehabilitation stay, including physician and therapist costs of opera	255 000
Search costs of the security agencies	20 000
Psychological damage	
Violent assault on 4 adults in their living space, plus the resulting anxiety in their retreat	4*1000+4*10 000
Time period while the offenders are on the run (14 days)	140
Psychotherapy for the 4 victims	4 000
Social damage	
2 weeks long escape from the police in the area with 74 523 inhabitants	14*10*74 523
Gunfight on the open road	100 000
Wounding of 3 passers-by and 2 police authorities	3*2000+2*2000

The total of all damages amounts to 10,941,360$. If the convicted person could not pay any of this, he would have to spend 1,094,136 hours in detention, or 125 years, at a Social Market Economy minimum wage of $10. Release from prison during his lifetime would only be possible for the robber if, while in detention, he develops an industrial property right capable of generating the amount of money, or owns companies that generate such a high profit. However, judges must specify a minimum sentence to be served in detention.

6 Clemency law[69]

In the clemency law, the Ministry of Justice determines who can issue pardons in individual cases and amnesties for entire groups of offenders, or when prisoners can shorten their imprisonment by committing suicide. The complete annulment of a sentence is only possible through negotiation in a committee with a subsequent referendum.

6.1 Pardon

In the case of a pardon, a sentence may be suspended, reduced or commuted to another sentence. The sentence and the guilt remain unaffected. Pardons can be issued by the people, the responsible judge and the prison management. The people can suspend a sentence via a veto quorum and a subsequent majority voting. Penalty payments then no longer have to be made and imprisonments no longer have to be served. The responsible judge can commute the sentence to another sentence if the victim has sufficiently recovered and the offender has sufficiently improved. The prison management can authorise furloughs and a day release for the inmate if he is on good behaviour.

6.2 Amnesty

Amnesty means either the waiver of claims of the opposing party or the waiver of sentence because the legal situation has changed. The plaintiffs can assert the waiver of claims of the opposing side against the convicted defendant before the responsible judge. Compensation payments are waived accordingly, but not fines or imprisonment. If the law changes to impunity, any further sentence that was based on the law is discontinued. The people decide on the amendment or repeal of a penal law, which is equivalent to an amnesty, in a voting. The people may, by a veto quorum against a sentence and a subsequent majority vote, remit the sentence and change it to an acquittal.

---

69 §251.4 Duration of detention: BV Art.173

Punished persons can apply for amnesty to the judge who once sentenced them if the law has changed in the meantime and the sentence could be more lenient as a result. If the application is rejected, prisoners can newly have their case reviewed in a revision case.

6.3 Suicide[70]

Prisoners are allowed to apply for suicide after 20 years of detention at the earliest. All prisoners sentenced to shorter imprisonments are not entitled to do so. For suicide, they are taken to a suicide cell[71] . All preliminary examinations and clarification interviews are conducted in the prisoner's cell. Only if the suicide takes place, the prisoner is taken by the guards of the Ministry of Justice to a hospital with a suicide cell The application may not be rejected, but in the case of a particular seriousness of the guilt, it may only be executed after a maximum of 30 years in total.

7 Penal forms

The penal law regulates which form of punishment is applied for which offence and guilt and how severe or lenient the sentence can be interpreted. The severity of the guilt, i.e. the immorality of the offender, determines the form of punishment, whereby combinations of forms of punishment are permissible. The severity of the guilt is determined by the judge and lay judge in the respective court proceedings for each individual case.

There are no suspended sentences, only compensation payments, fines, occupational bans, community service and forced labour in detention. The legal system provides very harsh sentences for violent offenders. There is no death penalty, but life-long labour for the survivors or victims. Sums of money are collected according to the law of execution by seizing and foreclosing on valuables through court bailiffs.

Statistics on the entire penal system and correctional system are

---

70 §4.1 Right to life: BV Art.10
71 Ministry of Family Affairs - 11.2 Suicide

kept and published with the help of the Court Directory. This is used to research recidivism rates and successful sentencing measures. The Ministry of Justice evaluates the data annually for the budget vote.

7.1 Compensation payments

Offenders must pay the compensation to the court immediately or in monthly instalments. The amount of the instalments is determined by the court, after inspecting the offender's work and asset situation. If an offender cannot pay the instalments, the instalments can be reduced until the monthly number is reached, which is the case when offenders work in detention. If offenders cannot pay even these instalments by gainful employment in an economic form, they must work off the remaining amount in detention. The court pays the compensation sums to the victims immediately and takes out a loan from the People's Bank[72] for this purpose. The interest rate on the loan corresponds to the inflation rate and must also be paid by the offender.

7.2 Monetary fine

Monetary fines are imposed for minor offences that did not involve violence against persons or things. The amount of the monetary fine is weighed up in court. If a fine is due 3 times in a row for the same offence, up to 48 hours of community service or up to 7 days of detention can be ordered by the court.

Those who cannot pay a monetary fine immediately or in instalments work off the amount in the nearest prison. Should one fail to show up for service, a warrant is issued and the defaulter is detained around the clock until the amount is paid.

72Ministry of Finance - 11 People's Bank

7.3 Occupational ban[73]

Persons who have wilfully caused damage to minors or dependents shall be given an occupational ban for professional or honorary service with minors or dependents. Entrepreneurs or shareholders who damage the general public through their company are no longer allowed to work in this industry. They must sell their company or their shares in it. Companies that have a business concept designed to damage the general public will be closed down.

7.4 Community service

Community service is imposed for offences without and with minor violence against persons or things in the possession of others committed by youths from the age of 10 to the age of majority or by adults for the first time. Community service is performed in Non-profit institutions or state institutions that serve social peace in the country. State institutions must report their need, Non-profits can do so. The report is made at the Ministry of Justice office in the local town hall. Community service can be imposed for up to one year with a maximum weekly work time of 40 hours. The convicts receive a work contract for which they are not paid, similar to an unpaid internship.

Performing community service should not endanger the convicted person's existing job. If this were the case, the convicted person has to state this in court and the judge calls the workplace and checks this.

Arrangements regarding existing gainful employment must be arranged by the convicted person himself. Firstly, one can choose institutions for community service that have different working hours. Secondly, it is possible to adjust the weekly working hours in agreement with the social institution and thus extend the duration of the employment contract for the completion of community service.

73§249.9 Criminal law: BV Art. 123c

7.5 Detention[74]

Anyone who is taken into custody, arrested or detained must be immediately informed of their rights in the coming proceedings of prosecution and court hearing. One has the right to immediately contact 2 relatives and retain a lawyer of one's election as legal counsel and to make statements only after consultation with him. No security agencies may be present during this arrangement, but it may take place in a locked room guarded by security agencies.

Deprivation of liberty is only permissible if laws have been violated and if laws provide for imprisonment for this. The violations of the law are determined in court proceedings and the sentence is also determined there. When depriving prisoners of their liberty, the prison system must adhere to the conditions of detention and administrative instructions laid down by the Ministry of Justice.

The Ministry of Justice is responsible for the necessary laws to regulate the execution of sentences and measures. This includes how prisons are built and how they are suitable for psychotherapy, work, education and training for prisoners. For minors, judges can order placement in a special school or upbringing camp where the imprisonment must be served.[75]

The length of imprisonment can range from one day to the end of life. Convicts are in the custody of the Ministry of Justice at this time of their lives, which is responsible for their safety and the safety of other humans before them. Data protection applies to prisoners in a special way because a lot of data has to be protected from access by prisoners.

7.5.1 Restriction of rights[76]

The punitive form of detention restricts the personal rights of the detainees. The right to personal freedom is restricted because there is no unrestricted freedom of movement. Prisoners are given the opportunity to move sufficiently to

---

74§32,1,2 Deprivation of liberty: BV Art.31, §249,3 Criminal law: V Art. 123
75Ministry of Education - 6 Special school, 5.17.7 Upbringing camps
76§84.8 Political civil rights, §4.2 Right to life: BV Art.10

keep their bodies healthy. Physical integrity is restricted if the prisoner himself uses physical force or escapes and therefore has to be temporarily incapacitated.

Detainees lose most of their civic participation rights. They are not given admission to the intranet through which they can interact with other humans. In order to be able to exercise their electoral and voting rights, voting booths are set up in the prison during election week.

7.5.2 Assessment of the duration of detention[77]

The amount of damages calculated by the court is divided by the applicable minimum wage in Social Market Economy[78] per hour. In detention, every hour counts. For example, a damage sum of material and psychological damage of 2400 Dollars, which is only to be punished with detention, would mean 10 days of detention with a minimum wage of 10 Dollars.

Apart from the monetary value of the sentence, a superior court judge may impose imprisonment until the end of life and exclude early release or furlough. The rights of the people and the prisoner in clemency law apply undiminished.

Imprisonment until the end of life is reserved for repeat offenders or offenders of violent crimes who are at high risk of recidivism, unless the value of the damage results in such a long period of imprisonment or the legislator explicitly provides for it. In order to be allowed to impose an imprisonment for life, security agencies and assessors must present evidence that expels the offender as extremely dangerous or that the offence will also cause damage to subsequent generations. 3 Therapists have to describe the offender in their assessors as not treatable and with a high risk of recidivism.

Should new scientific findings make therapy possible, offenders can request a newly conducted assessment. Should the therapy be approved, carried out and successful, gradual prison privileges can be granted under clemency law. The risk of liability if the offender recidivates is borne by the authorities that approved the prison privileges.

77§249,4,5 Criminal law: BV Art. 123a, §251,1,2 Detention period
78Ministry of Social Market Economy - 9.3.1 Minimum wage

7.5.3 Security guards

The guards are bound by the applicable laws on the execution of justice and are under the authority of the Ministry of Justice. In matters of staff representation, security forces of the Ministry of Security can help out the guards and vice versa. During service, the laws of the respective ministry apply and are presented to the staff on guard duty. Their knowledge is checked in an entrance test. Guards in prisons look after and monitor prisoners. They wear body cameras so that all their actions and processes are documented. The data is stored by radio on a computer in the prison and regularly transferred to the server of the Ministry of Justice. They may only be deleted once an imaged prisoner is living in freedom for one year or is dead.

7.5.4 Finance

Prisoners work off the monetary value of their sentence and receive no wages, only healthy food, safe work and warm accommodation and medical care. Prisoners have no money and cannot buy anything, not even cigarettes or similar consumer goods. Any income that the prisoner develops is either used to compensate his victims or to finance the prison operation.

The assets of prisoners must be transferred to their People's Bank account after the verdict. There it is invested in domestic government or corporate bonds on the People's Stock Exchange. The term of the bonds corresponds to the period of imprisonment. The annual interest is equal to the annual inflation rate. Only bank deposits and cash of the prisoner are invested. Whether he wants to sell, shut down or rent out his flat is up to him. Rental income is also invested with People's Bank. The aim is to keep the prisoner's assets constant, i.e. to compensate for inflation. After the imprisonment, the prisoner should not face financial ruin. Before detention, private insolvency may be filed in order to write off debts from the Free Market Economy.

Should a prisoner die in detention, his assets are used to pay off the remaining value of the compensation or sentence. The remaining assets are bequeathed in the testament.

7.5.5 Prison building

The Ministry of Justice administers the material equipment of the prisons as well as the budget, construction and real estate matters. It cooperates with the Ministry of Infrastructure on construction and maintenance work, and with the Procurement Office on equipment.[79] For equipment in security matters, only state enterprises are used as providers.

Prisons are mobile so that they can be placed as close as possible to where the prisoners work. They consist of transportable ISO containers. These containers are joined together to form a container cross. One container stands vertically in the centre. Around it, four containers are attached at 90° to each other at the end of one side. This standard module is stacked up to four times on top of each other, like a helix or a screw, so that the three upper floors are twisted towards each other. This way, each container floats freely and break-outs become more difficult. The lowest container cross, which rests on the floor, consists of a reception container with the only admission to the lift. The other three containers are used for the security staff, as a visiting room and as storage for commodities and operational containers for electricity, water, waste.

Prisons can vary in size. Depending on how many workers are needed, a corresponding number of detention centre buildings are built from container crosses. Each prisoner is given a single cell, so 12 prisoners can live in one prison building.

In the reception container, each detainee goes through a body scanner and is stopped for prohibited items. At the end of the reception container, there is a revolving door before the exit, followed by the two exit doors.

---

79 Ministry of Labour - 6 Procurement Office

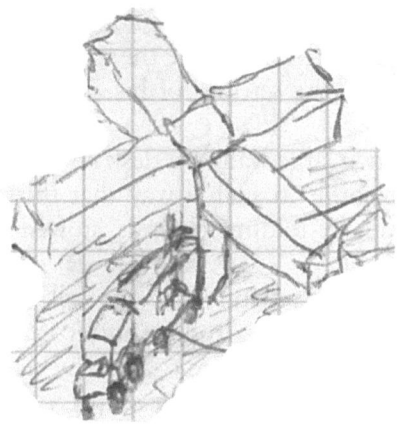

7.5.5.1 Cell

Each prisoner has an individual cell where they stay outside working hours. The cells are controlled once a week by the guards and cleaned by the prisoners.

The cell has an entrance and exit door with flaps for the hands, which is connected to the lift in the vertical container. The door slot at the bottom of the door is 35cm long and 10cm high. Laundry and food is pushed through here on a tray. Every 3rd day the prisoner gets a fresh towel and fresh clothes. Every 3rd day, after breakfast delivery, the dirty laundry is to be pushed through the door slit. In the camp, the guards keep the laundry, which is washed and delivered by a laundry of the Planned Economy or Social Market Economy.

On the opposite wall, the WC, shower and washbasin are next to each other in that order. At the threshold to the bathroom, the PVC floor is slightly recessed and has a drain under the shower head. The bathroom can thus be easily cleaned with warm water using the movable shower head. A wall of Plexiglas from the floor to the ceiling has a passage gap at the side of the washbasin and separates the bathroom from the rest of the cell.

On the wall in the bathroom, there are five ventilation slots at the upper end in an S-shape towards the ventilation slot on the outer wall of the container. There are grilles behind all the vents. In front of each interior ventilation slot are sliding doors that the prisoner can open and close himself. The entire cell is heated via underfloor heating and supported by the cell's hot water. The inmate can change the temperature of the floor heating himself in the settings of his cell in the multimedia system.

On one of the two large walls is a desk and a bed. Both pieces of furniture are built in such a way that they can be folded against the wall. A folding chair is stowed in the double bottom of the table.

The ceiling is the only window in the cell and offers a clear view of the sky. There is a roller shutter that can be closed between after 7 pm and before 6 am. The ceiling is made of bullet-proof glass with a safety wire insert. Then comes the intermediate shaft for the roller shutter, then another pane of bullet-proof glass where the multimedia unit is placed centrally. The beamers also serve as a light source. If there is a risk of damage, the roller shutter is automatically closed and locked.

7.5.5.2 Multimedia system

A multimedia system is housed in each cell. A ceiling camera monitors the room. It consists of three cameras, namely a 360° 3D camera, an infrared camera for night vision and a thermal imaging camera for the inmate's bodily functions. This eliminates the need for live monitoring.

Above the ceiling camera are LED beamers for the walls, below which is a beamer for the floor. This multimedia unit on the ceiling also contains all the sensors, for temperature, movement and a microphone for sounds and voice commands from the prisoner to the multimedia system of his cell. Speakers are embedded in the walls. All walls in the room are white and serve as a projection screen. Prisoners can virtually furnish their cell with pictures, plants, wall colours, additional rooms to meet virtual avatars, windows or "travel" to special places that were recorded with a 360° camera. The virtual windows never offer a direct view into a real environment, but into a virtual environment that was recorded somewhere at some time.

For example, you can wake up in the morning on the alpine

pasture. An alpine panorama with birdsong is shown all around the bed. If you don't wake up, the camera surveillance with motion detector notices and then a cow comes running next to the bed and from the loudspeakers comes a louder and louder "MUH!"

7.5.5.3 Hospitals

For health care, virtual doctor visits, real doctor visits and inpatient stays in special detention hospitals are carried out. The old prisons are partly converted into hospitals so that sick prisoners can be safely treated there as inpatients for a longer period of time. Free appointments are given to needy nationals from the Barter Economy or Free Market Economy without health insurance. Virtual doctor visits take place with a physician talking to the detainee's multimedia system in their cell via video telephony. Guards supervise the virtual doctor visits and are also subject to medical confidentiality. During real visits to the doctor, the physician comes to the prisoner's cell in person and has the necessary examination equipment with him. All examinations with special devices are carried out in the prison hospital.

7.5.6 Detention conditions

The conditions of detention are based on the enforcement plan, which is determined in the court proceedings. Should prisoners wish to object to the enforcement plan or to other conditions of detention, they can report a disciplinary complaint by filing a complaint with the public prosecutor's office.

All prisoners in a prison elect a prison advisory board. Every inmate can stand for election as a prison advisory board member and make a video of himself for this purpose, which is checked by the guards and viewed by other inmates. The election takes place digitally via the multimedia system when each prisoner is in his cell. The prison advisory board can be visited by inmates in the visiting room after work duty, by appointment, to talk about prison conditions. The meeting is monitored by the guards and recorded on video. The prison advisory board can make an appointment with the prison management at any time and contact the External Service of the Federal Moderator's Office.[?]

Imprisonments take place in mobile prisons with single cells. All prisoners have single cells so that there are no gangs, extortion or trade among the prisoners. In the cell, one can go to the toilet, take a shower, sleep, watch TV, listen to music, do sports or do all school, college and vocational degrees. Outside the cell, there are strict rules and close supervision. Prisoners only leave their cells to work or for medical treatment, which is not possible in the cell.

7.5.6.1 Relocation

If there is a need to balance occupancy due to overcrowding, the Ministry of Justice will arrange for the transfer of prisoners. Prisoners may only submit a motions for transfer if they can prove that they are particularly qualified for an advertised job. They can complete and submit the application via their multimedia system. Advertised activities indicate training courses and exercises that prisoners must complete in their cells in order to achieve the qualification.

7.5.6.2 Visit

Prisoners have 120 minutes visiting rights on their day off per week. The visiting room is divided into two halves by a central pane. Small compartments are divided off next to each other with partitions. A wired telephone receiver hangs on each partition, through which the prisoner and the visitor can talk to each other. The child support is recorded and automatically checked by a voice recognition software. If the algorithm detects violations, the corresponding text passages are transmitted to the guards.

7.5.6.3 Daily routine

The daily routine is similar for all inmates, but is mainly based on the inmate's working hours. In the morning, each inmate is automatically woken up by the multimedia system. The light slowly comes on in a light sequence from red to orange, yellow to white. Then a melody is played, which the prisoner can choose himself.

Hot food is delivered to the cell for breakfast, along with a packed cold lunch. This is followed by the way to the workplace and after the working day the way back to the cell. The guards put the collars on the prisoners before they leave the cell and take them off again before they enter. Serious offenders are additionally handcuffed, ankle-cuffed and put on opaque glasses until they are at the workplace. Guards take prisoners to and from the workplace. Supervision is provided for felons. The collars are used to automatically control the ban on talking and the observance of the movement radius. Back in the cell, hot dinner is provided. On rest days, only hot food is delivered in the morning along with a daily ration of cold food. For drinks, the prisoners use the tap water from their cell. For work, they fill the water bottle from the packed lunch.

Since the deliveries of the food pose a danger, all deliveries are screened in the reception container, distributed to the prisoners by the guards and collected again. Before leaving the reception container, the deliveries are screened again.

7.5.7 Speech ban

During duty periods, there is a ban on talking among the inmates and to other staff members on a duty station. The same applies to any stay outside the cell. The only exceptions are judges, lawyers, physicians and guards. On admission to prison, speech samples are taken. They are used to evaluate voice monitoring by computer and to know immediately who said what. The microphones in the collars permanently monitor the prisoner and his surroundings outside the cell. This is used to prevent collusion for escapes or smuggling. This is why the sign language lesson in the Knowledge Directory is turned off. If anyone is caught using sign language or any other sign language, it will be recorded by the cameras in the collar and brought to court. If communication is proven, the prisoner is sentenced to solitary confinement and transferred to another prison where the work area is under video surveillance.

Prisoners wear waistcoats outside their cells that say that no one is allowed to talk to them and that there is constant video surveillance. Inmates are allowed to talk to themselves, the computer voice or their lawyer or therapist in their individual cell via video telephony. The video telephony is recorded and evaluated in cases of criminal suspicion and used as evidence if necessary.

Prisoners are only allowed to talk to Ministry of Justice guards outside their cell. Workers on the construction site are allowed to give instructions to the prisoners, which the prisoners must carry out. If the prisoners do not want to carry out an instruction, they must explain this to the guard by voice request. He decides whether the instruction should be carried out or not, or whether the prisoner has to spend a day in solitary confinement for refusing to work. Working time is the only time prisoners are not in their solitary cells, apart from hospitalisation.

7.5.7.1 Accompanying voice

In the solitary cell, a parallel world of knowledge and civilised conversation is created. Inmates can talk there with a computer voice that has an answer to every question and asks questions itself or starts telling things. The vote is heard through a loudspeaker on the wall. A microphone is also built into the loudspeaker that recognises the prisoner's language and reacts to his speech. Prisoners can set this "accompanying voice" themselves. It can be set to be very present and wish them good morning as soon as they get up, ask them questions, mother them, ask if and how the food tastes. Or it can only react when spoken to and otherwise remain silent. Here, prisoners can also request psychological help if the accompanying voice no longer has any helpful answers to offer. The vote can be set male or female and display a certain temperament. A polite and educated tone is always spoken. If an inmate does not understand a word, he can ask the vote what the word means. The computer programme of the vote has access to the entire knowledge databases of the intranet. There are sentences that are spoken directly by the Minister of Justice, such as "Please work on yourself, do sports, get a degree or invent something groundbreaking. All this can help you give your life a positive meaning and leave something worth remembering for your posterity."

7.5.8 Collars

Prisoners wear a collar at all times outside the cell. The collar is used to protect persons working with the inmate and to prevent escapes and smuggling.

The collar for prisoners is produced by the People's Innovation Company[80] Intranet[81] . It includes a microphone, cameras, broadcasters and receivers for radio and satellite signals, a three-stage sleeping aid injection, a revolving multi-coloured LED light, a speaker, a body function sensor, a button and two batteries. All these devices are housed in a burch- and cut-proof casing that has a hinge on one side and a lock with a key and number combination on the opposite side. The collar is kept safe and charged by the guards while the prisoner is in the cell.

The body function sensor measures the inmate's exertion and is used for his safety from overexertion. The prisoner is allowed to view this data in his multimedia cell.

The button is used to call the security staff. Pressing this button triggers a voice request from the guard, which is displayed on the guard's Walkie-talkie.

The two batteries are housed separately from each other. One of them is smaller and specially secured. It sends an emergency signal as soon as the first battery threatens to run out. As soon as this second battery also threatens to run out, the sleeping aid injection is triggered and a final location message is sent

80 Ministry of Innovation - 10 People's Innovation Company
81 Ministry of Digital Affairs - 13 People's Innovation Company Intranet

to the satellite.

7.5.8.1 Monitoring devices

The microphone is used to monitor the inmate's voice. During detention, each detainee gives voice samples so that the voice recognition software recognises when the detainee is speaking. The four 180° cameras are distributed around the collar so that a 360° view is possible, which the prisoner could also achieve with a turn of the head and shoulders. Due to the strong fisheye effect, the camera viewing angle extends over the head and down to the floor.

The radio broadcaster can send a call signal to the guards and at the same time recognise the markers that have been set up to cover the inmate's movement area. The location of these markers is communicated to the inmate and the staff before the inmate starts work at a new location for the first time.

The radio receiver is used to allow guards to switch off the collar's voice software with their walkie-talkie. This walkie-talkie corresponds to the radios used by security forces[82] and is reprogrammed for use by guards. It serves as a control element for the collar and a communication tool for guards. It is manufactured on the People's Innovation Company Intranet. The satellite broadcaster continuously sends the inmate's position data to the Ministry of Security and Ministry of Justice so that the inmate can be located and the sleeping aid injection triggered in the event of an escape.

The satellite receiver is used on the one hand to have a second connection to the guard in order to call the guard to him. On the other hand, the receiver is used to receive the command for the sleeping aid injection.

7.5.8.2 Warning signals

The LED light is placed all around the collar so that it can be seen from all sides. Normally it is off, but when in use it can show 3 colours. Flashing green means that a voice request

---

82Ministry of Security - 4.2 Radio communication

has been sent to the guard. The light will not go out until the button on the guard's Walkie-talkie is released. Flashing red light means that the prisoner has spoken without permission. The flashing goes out as soon as the guard confirms "arrested" on the Walkie-talkie in the message for unauthorised speaking. Flashing blue light means that the detainee is outside his permitted range of movement and is thus automatically put on the wanted list.

The loudspeaker accompanies the red and blue lights with a shrill loud tone as a warning signal. In addition, the phrase "Attention, speaking ban disregarded" or "Caution! Escaped prisoner.".

7.5.8.3 Sleeping aid injection

The sleeping aid injection numbs the prisoner as soon as he uses force on persons or tries to escape. The sleeping aid is dosed specifically for each prisoner. Whether an injection by needles similar to a snake bite is necessary or a contact method similar to LSD is decided by the state of the art. The sleeping aid injection consists of three stages. The first stage is a mild anaesthetic that knocks the prisoner out for about 5 minutes. The second stage is a stronger anaesthetic, which puts the prisoner under anaesthesia. This lasts for about 60 minutes. The third stage is further episodes to maintain the effect of the second stage for as long as possible. Up to 16 hours are currently possible. The body function sensor protects against overdose. This measure is intended to be as safe for fellow inmates and as harmless to the inmate as possible. Therefore, numbing is only allowed until the inmate has been retrieved and restrained.

The first stage can be triggered by the guards via walkie-talkie as soon as there is violence against persons by the inmates. The second and third stages are only triggered in the event of an escape.

7.5.9 Punitive measures

In acute situations of physical violence, the guards will act with the necessary severity of all non-lethal weapons. Threats of physical violence or verbal attacks are warned once, then immediately punished as a breach of the rules with solitary confinement or punitive transfer. In addition, punitive measures apply to all custodial offences that are not part of the usual penal code. Other offences are brought before the courts.

In solitary confinement, the cell's media system is switched off and the shutters of the ceiling window are open and switched off. There is only cold water and no electric light. Food rations are reduced because there is no need to work 12 hours a day and stay in the cell permanently. Depending on how harsh or frequent a rule violation is found to be, days, weeks or months up to a year in solitary confinement are punished. Days in solitary confinement are always added to the prison term and do not replace it because no working hours are performed. Once a total of more than one month in solitary confinement has been imposed in a year, a judge must review these punitive measures by the judicial authorities on watch.

In order to prevent cooperation among the prisoners, one of the two parties is punitively transferred to another prison in case of communication contacts. Here, more unpleasant work has to be done. A transfer back is only possible once the other communication party has been released.

7.5.10 Work[83]

The Ministry of Justice takes over the labour and economic management of the prisons. Since a prison is mobile, it can be moved to where prisoners are to work.

Prisoners do work that would cost taxpayers' money or work that has a higher monetary value. All other ministries report their labour needs to the Ministry of Justice, which can be met by prisoners. This need must first be met in order to replace tax money.

83§251.3 Duration of detention

If the need is met, companies can register their demand. The wage for a prisoner is transferred to the Ministry of Justice and may not be more than 10% below the usual wage. If the wage offered by a company is so high that it exceeds the wage of a state worker, the prisoner works for the company and not for the state enterprise. This creates a profit because the company's wage is used to pay a state employee and the rest can be used in the state budget. For maximum yield, prisoners are used for jobs that match their level of education. Such appeals are higher paid and consequently replace more tax money.

The general principle is that prisoners are employed in private companies according to their potential to pose a risk to others. A 60-hour week with 12 hours of work per day and one day of rest per week applies to prisoners.

7.5.10.1 Costs and profits

Prisoners cost the state, or the taxpayer, food, lodging and security, but they create value that benefits the entire population. Prisoners create social value with their work and compensate their fellow human beings for the injustice they have done to them.

All prisoners receive the minimum wage, which is decisive for their length of imprisonment, even if they perform work that is remunerated higher than the minimum wage. Detainees do not receive money for their work in detention. Detainees work during detention to work off the monetary value of the damage they cause. Accordingly, the length of detention is measured. Refusal to work and illness are not counted towards the hours account, but the detention period is extended by this time. Regular rest days are counted towards the hourly account.

7.5.10.2 Educational level and risk potential

The prisoner's level of education and potential for danger will determine which job he or she is assigned to. Prisoners with a high level of education and a low potential for violence are employed in companies. Prisoners with a low level of education and a high potential for violence are used for jobs in the Ministry of Infrastructure. Accordingly, there are high and low security jobs. The inmates are sorted by offence, so that felons are with felons. Thus, petty criminals do not get contact with even more criminal persons. Depending on the seriousness of the inmates' offences, more or fewer guards are assigned per inmate. The staffing ratio is determined by the Ministry of Justice together with the guards. The Ministry of Security accompanies this process in an advisory capacity, because security forces at the place of residence have seen the potential danger of the offender in freedom.

All prisoners wear their collars during working hours to prevent escapes and assaults. At their place of work, they are monitored by microphone and camera, if necessary also by drone. If an inmate moves outside the permitted radius, the alarm is activated and the inmate is numbed by collar. Each work area is monitored by guards in person or from the control centre using the collars and the satellite-based and visibly marked out area.

7.5.10.3 Low level of safety

Low-security workplaces are companies and state enterprises that do not exclusively use prisoners for work and where prisoners work who do not need to be continuously supervised by guards. Supervisors or co-workers who are with the inmate on an ongoing basis can do the monitoring and are given an alarm transmitter and shackles in return. The prisoner can be taken to work by guards in the morning, picked up again in the evening and brought to the prison. The language ban can be relaxed if the situation allows it. Through the continuous image and sound recordings in the collar, all offences and statements are monitored, stored and automatically checked for violations.

If the prisoner moves outside the predefined area, stunning is automatically initiated. If the alarm is triggered, the guards at the control centre check the video images from the collar and assess the situation. They can make announcements over the loudspeaker or arrange for stunning, after which the prisoner can be restrained.

Prisoners with special qualifications, good conduct and low potential for violence are also allowed to work in the production of People's Innovation Company or Planned Enterprise[84] . This privilege is meant to be an incentive for further education in detention, even for those who have to serve very long imprisonments.

In the case of good conduct, a prisoner may apply to change jobs and thus be transferred to another prison. If qualifications are sought, a transfer is arranged for economic reasons.

7.5.10.4 High level of safety

Workplaces with a high level of security are construction sites and waste processing plants.[85] They are characterised by being well shielded so that surveillance is facilitated and escape is made difficult. Dangerous prisoners work in state-owned enterprises or in Planned Economy and Social Market Economy companies that have prepared for the use of dangerous prisoners. The preparations include fulfilling the necessary security precautions. Primarily, prisoners are employed as construction workers for factories, roads, harbours, flood control, Social Villages, recreation areas, terrain grading and other state construction projects. They are then part of the construction team in the Ministry of Infrastructure. All the foundation work is done by the most serious criminals, because at this stage of construction one can still overlook the entire construction site. Prisoners who are physically impaired have to collect rubbish, separate or do any other job in the state rubbish collection unit of the Ministry of Infrastructure that suits their physical needs.

84 Ministry of Planned Economy - 10.5 Planned Enterprise
85 Ministry of Infrastructure - 5.8 Construction Team, 4.9.2.2 Waste Processing Plants

7.5.11 Further education

Inmates can use the television, radio, music collection, library or self-learning programmes from the Knowledge Directory in their single cell. Security-related restrictions are applied. All content is also selected for its educational value. Therefore, not all radio and TV channels are on in prison. Content that glorifies violence is completely prohibited.

All programmes of the state television are available and all news of the private TV channels as well as selected broadcasts of the private television in which the information content is higher than the entertainment content. For example, these are documentaries, biographies, reports or such feature films, series or shows.

For the radio stations, attention is paid to a balance of all continental music from all continental radio stations. All free-to-air radio stations are accessible.

The music library contains all free music available worldwide. The library contains all e-books that are rights-free and available free of charge or that can be accessed via a state university licence. The data cannot be printed or transferred because the inmate has no storage media for this.

7.5.11.1 Training

Inmates can make limited use of the intranet to do training and further education. Those who have successfully passed a graduation can work in this occupational field if they have good conduct, provided that prisoners are employed in an appropriate activity. The inmate is then transferred if necessary. The Knowledge Directory is the only part of the intranet for which a prisoner has almost all the access rights that a free citizen has. The other parts of the intranet must be restricted in such a way that a prisoner cannot send or receive any news or other content with which he could communicate with escapees.

The Ministry of Education provides a corresponding version of the Knowledge Directory for prisoners.[86] The Ministry

---

86Ministry of Education - 12.4 Digitised education

of Digital Affairs provides a corresponding version of the educational game and produces the appropriate Virtual Reality glasses and other necessary extensions on the People's Innovation Company intranet and makes them available to the Ministry of Justice.[87] None of these glasses have WLAN, but they are connected to the cell ceiling by cable. The cable can be unwound to such an extent that the prisoner can move around the entire cell. These glasses have specially encrypted secret intranet software so that the prisoners cannot communicate unnoticed.

All educational content is available digitally and all activities can be simulated using Virtual Reality glasses and sensor clothing. It should be possible to take any final exam from the cell and to work through the learning material using Virtual Reality glasses and sensor clothing. For this purpose, the software of the Virtual Reality glasses recognises every object in the room that can be used as a prop. The transparent Virtual Reality glasses are used to move the cell's furnishings to the correct position, and then put on the opaque Virtual Reality glasses if necessary. In this way, an inmate virtually bakes a cake for pastry training, for example. Those who have passed all the performance records receive a certificate. With this, after detention, one can register for the real final exam that matches the certificate and no longer has to attend classes. If the further training enables the qualification for another job in detention, the prisoner can be transferred accordingly.

7.5.12 Psychotherapy

On the one hand, detention is used to get offenders into gainful employment in order to cover costs and make profits. On the other hand, detention is also used to provide therapy to the offenders during the time. Psychotherapy is carried out by professionals and digitally. To start with, the prisoner takes digital tests, on the basis of which the algorithm of the psychotherapy game[88] and the professionals draw up a therapy

---

87 Ministry of Digital Affairs - 15.8 Educational game, 13.6.9.1 Virtual reality glasses, 13.6.9 Extensions
88 Ministry of Digital Affairs - 15.6 Psychotherapy Game

plan.

Inmates can request a psychologist consultation in their multimedia programme. To do this, they go to the start menu and select "Book psychologist". They will then be shown free appointments. After their service, they can talk to a psychologist via video telephony. Some prisoners also get this prescribed by the court.

7.5.12.1 Forms of therapy

First, there is personal biographical therapy, in which traumatic life events are processed. This is what the psychotherapy game is designed for, which accompanies the therapy sessions with a mental health professional. The professional can give specific missions as tasks until the next session and then talk about them and evaluate results.

Secondly, there is social therapy, in which offenders learn to behave in a legal and friendly manner. This form of therapy is implemented by the computer programme in the single cell, where the inmate creates his own virtual roommates who speak to him over loudspeakers and whose image is projected on the walls of the cell. These roommates engage in legal activities, always face the prisoner and are friendly to him. If he is angry with them, they are sad and express their feelings.

Thirdly, there is counter-extremism in prison, whereby offenders do not come into contact with other offenders to radicalise each other, but are separated from each other. In addition to the solitary cells and the ban on talking, there are also different prisons and workplaces for different serious offences.

In addition, a questionnaire is used to record whether prisoners have radical religious, cultural or political attitudes. As a form of therapy, a media package is put together that the prisoners have to consume in order to inform themselves as comprehensively as possible about the affected topic. In therapy sessions, the content and opinions on it are reviewed. The point is to learn to understand other opinions, not to have to accept them. However, prisoners should be told when they may meet with rejection in society with an extreme opinion.

8 Criminal law of the ministries[89]

All ministries can enact laws that impose sentences on acts that fall within their remit. Penal laws of the ministries are formulated in voting with the Ministry of Justice in order to be able to guarantee proportionality and the realisation of fundamental rights. In particular, sentences are due whenever the state or citizens violate fundamental rights. Ministries have the duty to enact corresponding penal laws in order to prevent or punish violations of fundamental rights.

8.1 Ministry of Labour

8.1.1 Confidentiality of the Company Auditing Agency

Police officers check the work of the auditors of the Company Auditing Agency.[90] Breach of confidentiality is punishable by at least 5 years' detention or by the measured amount of damages determined in court proceedings.

8.1.2 Bribery

Police officers check the work of the auditors of the Company Auditing Agency.[91] Bribery in the audit of companies or ministries and draft budgets is punishable by an imprisonment of at least 5 years. The charges initially result in suspension for the auditors. The court proceedings will decide whether they will be released or how long the imprisonment will be. All court hearings are conducted in public as long as no company secrets are jeopardised.

---

89 §36 Realisation of fundamental rights: BV Art.35
90 Ministry of Labour - 20.7.6.1 Company Auditing Agency work audit
91 Ministry of Labour - 20.7.6.1 Company Auditing Agency work audit

8.1.3 Corporate criminal law[92]

The purpose of corporate criminal law is to be able to combat white-collar crime under criminal law. While persons can usually be held responsible under criminal law, legal persons in the form of organisations, unifications, companies and other partnerships can be held responsible under corporate criminal law. In the regular audits of the Company Auditing Agency, compliance with corporate criminal law is checked on an ongoing basis. Legality auditors are responsible for reporting violations immediately.[93] Judges decide which offences result in which sentences after court proceedings.

Corporate criminal law also applies to state enterprises, but is supplemented by the official liability of politicians.

8.1.3.1 Violations

Offences are acts that endanger the general welfare and have the following characteristics. Entrepreneurs are prosecuted under corporate criminal law if they evade taxes, set up dummy companies and subsidiaries in order to shift losses there and thus render these companies insolvent or to avert liability from the parent company.

The same applies if they violate labour rights, put employees or customers under psychological pressure against their will, employ undeclared workers, pay wages below the collective labour agreement or the minimum wage, or allow employees to be lied to on duty by colleagues or superiors. Official lying concerns any activity that happens within working hours or arrangements that affect the service.

It is also a sentence to manufacture products that break according to plan faster than necessary, and to suppress patents or innovations that would enable humanity to raise its standard of living.

Suppression of innovation occurs when employees or outsiders report new work processes or inventions to a company that are not implemented despite proven effectiveness and when

---

92 §148.7 Principles of taxation: KV Art.104
93 Ministry of Labour - 20.7.6 Legality auditor

the inventors are not compensated. Suppression of patents occurs when a company buys innovative patents without implementing them, only to protect its own backward technology.

Companies are also penalised if they act with gross negligence, fraudulently deceive and intentionally create negative externalities.

8.1.3.2 Sentences

Sentences for companies differ from sentences for persons as follows. Monetary fines and compensation payments are financed from the company account and paid out as usual to the responsible court or to injured parties.

Imprisonment for persons is imposed on the managing director and the board of directors. Imprisonment for companies means partial or total temporary nationalisation without consideration. During this time, the business consultants of the Company Auditing Agency[94] run the company in voting with the employees.

The occupational ban or confiscation means the expropriation of a company without consideration for the owners. Depending on the employees' complicity, the company is sold. If the employees are not guilty, the company is transferred to the employees if they pay a redemption sum that is 10% above the costs incurred by the state due to the criminal company. The redemption sum can be paid in instalments, which are due as soon as profits are made. If the company is unprofitable or in debt, it is given as a gift to the workforce. If they refuse the gift, the company is closed. If the employees are partly to blame, the company is auctioned off to the highest bidder or closed down.

---

94 Ministry of Labour - 20.7.7 Business consultant

8.1.3.3 Ruinous circular economy

What is punishable is a circular economy of companies that produce inland or abroad at low wages, provide cheap goods and services that low-wage earners can just about afford, and still skim off profits. This circular economy makes the rich richer and the poor poorer, which in the long run destroys the domestic economy.

As a punitive measure, wages and prices can be changed by a court judgment. In finding and justifying the sentence, judges must observe the following principles. Products should be cheap because productivity is high, not because wages are low. This strengthens domestic consumption. Products can be expensive if they are innovative. Products should deliver what manufacturers promise customers. Products should last a long time, at least 5 years. Companies should not produce externalities in order to lower their production costs and thus burden humans and nature. Instead, production costs should be reduced through innovations.

8.1.3.4 False promises

Superiors are not allowed to promise their subordinates anything in return for a wage sacrifice, extra work or other work that is less beneficial to the subordinate, and then not honour it. Such incidents are queried in the annual questionnaires of the Company Auditing Agency in all domestic companies with salaried employees.[95] Superiors who commit this offence must continue to do the work, but will only receive as much pay as the subordinate to whom they made false promises. The time limit for this depends on the amount of damage.

8.1.3.5 Damage to humans and nature

If companies cause damage to humans or nature without having drawn attention to it beforehand and included compensation in the price of their service, they are penalised. The Company Auditing Agency's health auditors continuously

---

95 Ministry of Labour - Compliance with labour law

check compliance with the requirements.[96]
The first sentence is to repair the damage within one year and to pay compensation. The second sentence is if the damage has not been remedied in the next audit next year. Now the company must invest all its profits in research that will prevent damage. If after 5 years the damage continues, all domestically affected companies must close down and all injurious ones may no longer be offered and used domestically. Remaining company capital is used for research and marketing of harmless comparable products as well as for compensation of humans and nature.

8.1.3.6 Waste disposal

If companies cannot cover disposal costs of their waste because they have not priced it in, even if these companies are or have been sold, all company owners of that period of waste production will be expropriated until the disposal costs are covered. The affected companies will be nationalised and transitionally managed by the Company Auditing Agency's business consultants.[97] All managers during whose duty period the waste was produced and who ordered the production of the waste will be liable with their private assets and, if they cannot meet the costs, will have to go into detention until they have worked off the balance. Once all disposal costs have been covered, owners are released from detention and given back their companies.

8.1.4 Insolvency delay

When companies become insolvent, they must report it immediately to their Ministry of Economy. If the report is not made, criminal proceedings will be instituted for delaying insolvency. The debtor is then liable with his private assets and must pay a residual debt in detention if he cannot pay it. The debtor works in detention at the minimum wage until the full

96Ministry of Labour - Health auditor
97Ministry of Labour - Implementation of the expropriation

amount has been worked off.

If insolvency occurs as scheduled, the procedure differs in the economic forms. In the event of attachment, the Company Auditing Agency's legality auditors enforce insolvency law.[98]

No debts can be incurred in the Planned Economy. Since all work is invoiced in hours, a consideration must be worked off. In the Social Market Economy, insolvency insurance applies and the companies are accompanied by the business consultants of the Company Auditing Agency in the insolvency proceedings. In the Barter Economy, the debtor must work off the outstanding performance for his creditor. In the Free Market Economy, the declaration of insolvency applies and for creditors the default on payment, against which one can insure oneself in the Free Market Economy.

8.1.5 General Terms and Conditions (GTC)

GTC may be a maximum of 2 pages long and must sufficiently describe the company's constitution. The customer must be able to understand what kind of company he is doing business with here and what risk he is taking. The legality auditors of the Company Auditing Agency check this regularly.[99] Violations are punishable by a monetary fine of 10% of the profits of the previous year.

8.1.6 Right to have fun at work

Every worker has the right to have fun at work.[100] If the opportunity to have fun fails to materialise, a monetary fine equivalent to one month's salary of the company's best-paid employee becomes due. The legality auditors check the measures and punish violations.[101]

---

98 Ministry of Labour - 20.7.6.11 Enforcement of insolvency law
99 Ministry of Labour - 20.7.6.8 Compliance with labour law
100 Ministry of Labour - 16.5 Fun at work
101 Ministry of Labour - 20.7.6.8 Compliance with labour law

8.1.7 Insurances

Insurance law is the responsibility of the ministries of labour and economy.[102] Insurance operated by ministries is also subject to insurance law. Insurance companies determine the contributions and benefits and when they are due. Anyone who pays insufficient contributions can lose insurance cover. Anyone who fraudulently obtains insurance benefits is liable to prosecution and will be fined 2 times the amount of the fraudulent insurance benefit. In the case of multiple offences, 0.5 times the amount will be served in detention. Additional sentences under corporate criminal law are possible.

8.1.8 Finance economy

Financial market law and securities law are the responsibility of the ministries of labour, finance and economics. Depending on which of the six ministries is affected, the corresponding department in the court takes over financial jurisdiction. The ministries determine who may issue which security where and which rights and obligations are binding. The Financial Supervisory Authority[103] conducts the necessary examinations and thus provides for an initial taking of evidence, which in case of suspicion leads to indictment. Anyone who cheats or deceives in securities trading is sentenced to community service in addition to compensation payments for a first offence, and to imprisonment for repeated offences. Additional sentences under corporate criminal law are possible.

8.2 Ministry of Foreign Affairs

8.2.1 Continental Business Law

In cooperation with the continental ministries of economy and labour, continental company law is agreed to which all forms of enterprise must adhere. The exclusion of trade with

---

102 Ministry of Labour - 10.2.4 Citizens' Insurance, 18.3.2 Insurance Supervisory Authority, Ministries of Economy - Finance economy
103 Ministry of Labour - 18.3 Financial Supervisory Authority

certain economic forms is regulated in continental company law. Violations of this will result in import or export bans.

8.2.2 International business law

In the jurisprudence of foreign trade law, the responsible nation's courts follow the international trade law of the responsible United Nations commission UNCITRAL (United Nations Commission on International Trade Law). The International Oil Pollution Compensation Funds (IOPC Funds) are used to compensate persons and regions who have been victims of environmental damage caused by oil. Companies or states that do not comply with international law are excluded from trade with the inland.

8.2.3 Ban on spying

The law on international intelligence services stipulates that no foreigner secret service is active inland and, in return, no domestic secret service exists either. Violations result in the imprisonment of the spies. Espionage is punishable by a minimum of 5 years detention. Diplomatic relations with the responsible state are suspended.

8.2.4 Air traffic

The Ministry of Foreign Affairs regulates overflight and landing rights with foreign private companies and state authorities in aviation law, which all pilots must abide by. Violations are punished with the withdrawal of overflight rights or landing rights.

8.2.5 Intergovernmental punitive measures

In order to punish states or companies and persons of foreign states, the following intergovernmental punitive measures can be used. They are only used if the foreign states are not willing to cooperate. The punitive measures consist of bans on the entry or exit of certain persons or all nationals of the affected state, a visa requirement, bans on the import or export of goods and services, the prohibition of trade and business activities of foreigners in the inland or domestic companies in the affected foreign country, the seizure of real or monetary assets of nationals or companies of the affected foreign country, and the partial or total severance of diplomatic relations. War is not an interstate punitive measure. A military attack from abroad is followed by defence from within the country.

8.3 Ministry of Education

8.3.1 Education and research law

The Ministry of Education sets the law of education and research for state and private education and research institutions. If institutions do not comply with the laws affecting them after the Company Auditing Agency has reported the deficiencies to them and the deadline for rectification has expired, they are penalised. The sentences may include monetary fines, nationalisation or closure. State institutions cannot be nationalised, but the Ministry of Education can be forced to correct the deficiencies within a time limit set by the court or the institution must be closed.

8.3.2 Right to education

Nationals and minors have a right to education and may bring a claim under state law if the necessary education is not available to them. Children up to the age of 10 are entitled to attend an educational institution appropriate to their age within a radius of 5 kilometres. If this is not possible, the responsible municipality must pay a compensation equivalent to the cost to the parents or provide a transport service.

8.4 Ministry of Digital Affairs

8.4.1 Digital crime

To combat computer crime under criminal law, the Ministry of Digital Affairs regulates criminal law for the internet and intranet. The misuse and theft of data is punished in the same way as the theft or misuse of other property belonging to third parties. Illegal trade and gambling will be treated equally in real and digital terms and will be punished by monetary fine or detention. Communicative offences, such as defamation or bullying, are equated in real and digital terms and are punishable by community service or detention. The severity of the offence is primarily based on the number of persons who commit communicative offences and the size of the group of persons who learn about them. The use of spam, viruses, Trojans and other harmful software is considered an attack with a digital weapon and is punishable by community service or detention. Advertising may not take up more than 10% in the digital space, otherwise a monetary fine is due that is at least 2 times the advertising revenue.

8.4.2 Data access

Access to data must be authorised by the owner or provided for by law. Anyone who collects data and states a false purpose for doing so is liable to 12 months detention. All data retrievals from the People's Computer must be recorded in an access log[104] . Data queries without an access log are punishable by community service if infrequent, and detention if very frequent. In case of doubt, every access can be questioned by the citizen and the purpose is indicated. If, in the opinion of the citizen, this access is not justified in order to achieve the stated purpose, a charge of unauthorised data access can be filed in court. The State may retrieve all data from the People's Computer, but nevertheless all access must be recorded in the Access Directory and the use of the data is bound by law. Temporary exceptions apply to investigations.

---

104 Ministry of Digital Affairs - 7.5 Access Directory

8.4.3 Anonymisation

Anyone who does not want to be mentioned or shown has the right to have relevant data about themselves deleted immediately. Anyone who resists the request for deletion or shares or stores data to be deleted is liable to at least 12 months' detention.

Anyone who does not want to be mentioned or pictured at public events can download a QR code from the Ministry of Digital Affairs website and visibly affix it at a maximum distance of 25 centimetres from the boundary of their face. Digital cameras recognise the code and the face and automatically black out the affected person's face. Users of analogue cameras are obliged to blacken afterwards.

8.4.4 Manipulation of opinion on the intranet

If posts or comments are repeatedly published on the intranet that are derogatory, negative, derogatory or bad about a matter, this is considered to be opinion manipulation. Authors will be required to delete affected statements or to further elaborate to support their opinions with new evidence. A monetary fine will be imposed for further dissemination of deleted statements. If the opinion or deed of a particular person has been denigrated, that person receives compensation amounting to 1% of all monetary fines. The originator must apologise for his or her actions in the same place and present the facts correctly.

If companies or associations engage in such opinion manipulation, their profiles may be blocked for one week in the event of a first-time violation. In case of a repeated violation, the profile will be deleted and the company or association will be closed. If it can be proven that persons were forced to publish statements in their name which had to be in the interest of the company, criminal proceedings for manipulation of opinion and coercion will be brought against the superior person responsible for the coercion.

8.5 Ministry of Family Affairs

8.5.1 Care

The law on care regulates which duties are connected with the duty of supervision for minors and which risks are decisive for child development. It regulates how the duty of supervision can be transferred to whom and what this means for personal liability. Anyone who violates the requirements for the best interests of the child when professionally caring for minors is liable to prosecution and must expect community service, occupational ban or imprisonment.

8.5.2 Family and marriage

Family law is considered to be overarching law that has parts in all areas of law. Civil law is affected when parents fight in court. Criminal law is affected when parents commit offences against their children or their children under the age of criminal responsibility. State law is affected when the state owes benefits to families or demands benefits from families. Constitutional law is affected when principles of parenthood, childhood and the concept of family are determined.

Marriage and divorce are considered part of family law. In the course of marriage, both partners must observe the pension equalisation law and conclude a marriage contract that regulates the pension equalisation during the marriage and in the event of a divorce. In the event of a divorce, maintenance law is applied to clarify in court what payments parents must make who care for their child only partially or not at all. The maintenance law provides a table that can be used to determine the maintenance amounts according to the years of the child's life and the parents' income level. If both parents take care of the child in equal shares, no maintenance payments are made. The care time is determined by the judge in consultation with the parents and children for each parent as a percentage.

8.5.3 Age of criminal responsibility[105]

Children do not reach the age of criminal responsibility until they are 10 years old, and parents have an unrestricted duty of supervision until then. Parents are liable for their child's criminal offences until the age of 10. In the case of criminal offences, adult criminal law applies to both parents. The sentence is divided equally between the two parents. Fines can be paid in instalments and imprisonments can be served by both parents consecutively. If the parents are sentenced to imprisonment, the child under the age of criminal responsibility has to go to the Social Village's special school and live in the children's home for 6 months. There, behavioural problems are observed, documented and suitable offers are developed to strengthen the child's strengths.

In the court proceedings, the judge considers whether it is better to have the child or all of the parents' children taken into care by the Youth Welfare Office or whether one parent alone or both parents should be detained. Taking minors into custody results in their placement in a children's home of a Social Village until a foster family or the natural parents take over the care of the child again.[106]

8.5.4 Child welfare endangerment

A child's well-being is endangered by anyone who violates the rights of the child.[107] A serious threat to the welfare of a child is committed by someone who inflicts physical, psychological or sexual violence on a child.

Anyone who suspects that a child's well-being is at risk must report this to the police, who are then entitled to carry out unannounced visits and undercover observations as well as to examine and question the child. If the suspicion persists and is confirmed by the paediatrician, further unannounced visits by the police are possible. Depending on the severity of the offence, various measures will be taken.

---

105 §179,4 Promotion of children and youths: BV Art.67
106 Ministry of Planned Economy - 18.1.7 Children's House
107 Ministry of Family Affairs - 8.1 Children's rights

8.5.4.1 Minor offences

If parents commit the child welfare endangerment, they must register at the Town Hall Office of the Ministry of Family Affairs for a newly examination for the parenting licence. If labourers commit the child welfare endangerment, they receive a warning and a ban on contact with the child. If they do it again, they will be terminated and reported to the police.

8.5.4.2 Serious offences

If there is a serious risk to the welfare of the child, pre-trial detention for defendants is ordered. In the first instance, the endangering parent should have to leave the family before the child has to leave the family through custody. If the parents live together, both parents always endanger the child's welfare. This is due to the fact that the supposedly uninvolved parent has not fulfilled his or her duty of supervision and his or her child did not have sufficient trust to confide in the parent. If the parents live separately, only one parent can be accused of endangering the welfare of the child.

If only one parent is accused of endangering the welfare of the child, the children live with the non-accused parent. The children of the parents may decide whether they want to be cared for by the non-accused parent or whether they want to live in the children's home[108] of a Social Village until the court proceedings are over. If possible, the child at risk should always be allowed to stay with his or her siblings if he or she wishes to do so. If children cannot speak yet, they have to go to the children's home, but can then be accompanied by the non-accused parent.

8.5.4.3 Taking into custody

If both parents are accused, all children of these parents are taken into custody by the police and taken to the nearest children's home.

The parents are remanded in custody until the Municipal

108 Ministry of Planned Economy - 18.1.7 Children's House

Court has heard the case and clarified the care issue in its judgement. The remand can be carried out in a Social Village so that parents can practise child-friendly handling on their own children under the guidance of a specialist in the children's home. However, the children must agree to the handling beforehand.

8.5.4.4 Detention

The person who, after being informed by the authorities, persistently endangers the best interests of the child, or who has committed at least one serious offence endangering the best interests of the child, is liable to detention. The imprisonment is determined by the severity of the offence and ranges from 9 months to life imprisonment.

If one parent is convicted in family court proceedings, he or she is liable to detention and the children remain with the other parent. The children have the right to move into the children's home at any time. If the parents are convicted, they are liable to detention and their children are taken into state custody. The children can live in the children's home or opt for foster care[109] . After the parents' imprisonment, the children can decide whether they want to live with their parents again.

8.5.5 Juvenile criminal law

Juvenile criminal law is applied to persons between the ages of 10 and 18. It provides for lighter sentences and focuses on therapy and educational measures. Prison sentences can be shortened and replaced by attending an upbringing camp for several weeks or moving in to a Social Village for the duration of the imprisonment. Youths must then report daily to the police station in the Social Village, attend the special school for the behaviourally disturbed and perform community service in social institutions in the Social Village. In court proceedings involving minors, their identity must be anonymised.

---

109 Ministry of Family Affairs - 7.6.5 Adoption

8.5.6 Youth Protection Act

Allowing one's own children to violate the Youth Protection Act is punishable by law. Parents or guardians must perform community service, pass a re-examination of the parenting licence or, in the case of multiple violations, an imprisonment will follow. Violations of the Youth Protection Act by youths between the ages of 10 and 18 are punished by attending an upbringing camp for several weeks. The number of weeks can range from 7 days to 6 weeks, depending on the severity of the violation.

8.5.7 Sexual offences

Sexual offences are all sexual acts that have taken place against the will of a participant. In case of doubt, the sexual partners are obliged to declare their mutual consent at the Registry Office. Before sexual acts involving the use of force or coercion, a mutual declaration of consent must be submitted to the Registry Office. Before sexual intercourse between minors and adults within the maximum age difference of 3 years, this declaration of consent is mandatory. Only in the case of a declaration of consent at the Registry Office is a sexual offence legally excluded.

The Sexual Offences Act provides for a more detailed psychological assessment and therapy of the offenders. In the case of high risk of recidivism and failed therapy with established inability to undergo therapy, the Sexual Offences Act provides for harsher sentences. The harsher sentences lead either to longer imprisonments or to surgical amputation or mutilation of the offender's sexual organ. Offenders can choose one of the two options. If they opt for surgery on the sexual organ, they have the right to donate sperm or eggs beforehand and to use them for themselves later.

8.5.8 Public nuisance

Being naked in public or performing sexual acts on oneself or with the consent of others is not a public nuisance. For hygienic reasons, human excreta should only be excreted in closed containers, cloths or similar, so that they can be disposed of afterwards in the residual waste. Humans and their natural drives are not taboo and not a public nuisance. Only those who want to do damage to others cause a public nuisance. As long as no one in the visible vicinity objects, the sexual urge or the need to relieve oneself is not a public nuisance.

Continuation despite objection is punishable by a monetary fine of 20 Dollars or more and, in particularly serious cases, 2 months' detention. Sexual abuse or disregard for faecal hygiene remain separate offences, but the penalty for the accused can be increased if they have taken place in public.

Spit and urine may only be discharged into unsealed soil. Excrement must be buried to a depth of at least 30 cm if it cannot be discharged into a toilet within a radius of 2 kilometres. Violations are punishable by a monetary fine of 50 Dollars, in repeated cases the fine doubles each time.

8.5.9 Doping in competitive sport

The Ministry of Family Affairs arranges for doping tests of competitive athletes by the health auditors of the Company Auditing Agency. Athletes, coaches and doctors who use doping in competitive sports, which prohibits doping, are banned for life.

8.6 Ministry of Finance

8.6.1 Taxes[110]

The tax law[111] provides for the management of taxes and their verification[112] . Those who do not manage taxes or manage them insufficiently must pay back 2 times the number for the first offence. In case of further offences, 2 times the amount must be paid back and 0.5 times the amount must be worked off in detention.

Whether taxes have been sufficiently paid is decided in case law in case of doubt. If the tax laws are not sufficient to determine sufficient tax payment in an individual case, judges create a precedent with this individual case, i.e. a judgement that all subsequent judgements are guided by. The electorate and the Minister of Finance are free to incorporate fundamental parts of the ruling into a law.

8.6.2 Public finances

Financial constitutional law[113] regulates state budget management. Misdeclared amounts or misappropriated funds result in criminal proceedings, which can be concluded with occupational ban, fine or detention.

8.7 Ministry of Health

8.7.1 Pollution

Pollution occurs when things that are harmful to the environment are not used or disposed of properly and in accordance with the regulations. The extent of the damage determines the amount of the sentence. On the one hand, it is calculated how high the subsequent disposal costs are.

110 §148.7 Principles of taxation: KV Art.104
111 Ministry of Finance - 5 Tax policy
112 Ministry of Labour - 20.7.1 Tax auditor
113 Ministry of Finance - 7 Budget consolidation, 8 State revenues, 9 State expenditure

This amount quantifies the amount of the compensation payments. The duration of the natural degradation process at the site of the improper disposal determines the length of the imprisonment. The sentence is measured by how long it would have taken if the waste had naturally degraded on site. The direct environment in which the item was disposed of is taken as the basis. Air, water, soil, sealed surface or thicket can mean different degradation times for different items. In any case, if the degradation process takes longer than a current average human life, a blanket life imprisonment is imposed. If pollution has an effect for longer than 30 years, the offence of negligent bodily harm to the next generation is considered to have been committed and leads to a doubling of the imprisonment.

The ministries of health and justice provide for criminal law against environmental crime. If companies commit environmental pollution, the persons responsible have to go to detention and the company has to remit its profits to the ministries of health and infrastructure until the pollution is reversed by the ministries and all these costs are covered. To determine the amount, the costs of cleaning and disposal are used. Since this is not the actual task of these ministries, a penalty payment is due that corresponds to the disposal costs. This penalty payment is additional and must be paid into the treasury by the budget vote after next.

Pollution is a criminal offence that can be reported to the police and is detected by the security forces. The health auditors[114] detect pollution at ministries and companies. The auditors of the Company Auditing Agency for Health, Technology, Business and Innovation check the cost of disposal and the performance of ministries until the damage is repaired.

114Ministry of Labour - 20.7.2 Health auditor

8.8 Ministry of Infrastructure

8.8.1 Mining law

Those who engage in mining, surface mining or well digging without a permit from the Ministry of Infrastructure are punished. The sentences provide for dismantling, restoring the original state, and imprisonment for at least 6 months.

8.8.2 Building law

Anyone who builds on a plot of land without permission from the Ministry of Infrastructure[115] will be penalised. The sentences provide for deconstruction, which restores the original condition. In case of repetition, community service and detention are also provided for.

8.8.3 Disposal of contaminated sites

The disposal of contaminated sites is handled and paid for by the originators. If neither the originator personally nor the company causing the pollution is able to do so, even by paying in instalments, criminal proceedings are initiated. Entrepreneurs are expropriated without compensation and all earnings from the company are used to cover the disposal costs. Moreover, originators are liable with all their private assets. If this is not enough, they work off the balance in detention.

8.8.4 Energy

Anyone who causes damage through negligent or improper handling of energy installations shall be ordered to pay compensation. Nuclear energy may only be used for peaceful purposes. The production of any nuclear weapons is punishable by life imprisonment and expropriation. Nuclear energy and any other source of energy may only be operated if it does not produce waste materials that cannot be naturally decomposed

---

115 Ministry of Infrastructure - 5.4 Building permits

after 30 years, even according to technical procedures. Running power plants that do not meet these requirements must use all the profits they generate to produce alternative energy sources that do meet the requirements. Once the energy output has been replaced by renewable energy sources, shutdown and decommissioning will take place. If the Company Auditing Agency determines that there is an increased risk of danger to public safety, the forced shutdown will take place.

8.8.5 Criminal traffic law

Anyone who violates traffic law[116] or negligently or wantonly endangers or damages other road users will be punished. Depending on the severity of the guilt and the frequency of the offences, the sentences range from monetary fines to driving bans to the revocation of driving or flying licences. The Ministry of Infrastructure compiles a catalogue of fines and a register for this purpose. In the register, points are awarded for offences. When certain point values are reached, a driving ban is imposed for a limited period of time. If the maximum number of points is reached, the driving or flying licence is revoked. Depending on the severity of the offence, the revocation may be for a limited period of time or for life.

8.8.6 Admission to electricity and broadband

For consumer protection in the energy sector, lack of admission despite payment is penalised. If electricity, internet or telephone providers leave a customer without service when changing providers or during the term of a contract, those affected are entitled to a lump sum compensation of 2000 Dollars per day. The group of affected persons is determined in court proceedings.

Unauthorised use of other people's frequencies is punishable by at least 2 years' detention.

Unauthorised use of the intranet frequencies is punishable by at least 5 years' detention.

116Ministry of Infrastructure - 8.2 Traffic law

8.9 Ministry of Innovation

8.9.1 Product piracy

To combat product piracy, compensation payments are due as soon as inventor's rights, trademark rights, design rights, copyrights or patent rights are infringed.[117] Illegal copies must be destroyed immediately after the judgement, unless the property right holder allows subsequent licensing. Anyone who nevertheless uses unauthorised copies will be punished with a monetary fine or community service.

8.9.2 People's Innovation Company bankruptcies

When a People's Innovation Company has reached the loss limit of the construction costs, responsible politicians on the company's board have to assume official liability and are dismissed. The company is closed down. The People's Innovation Company Fund[118] bears the losses incurred minus all sales proceeds.

8.9.3 Procrastination of innovation

When companies or persons withhold innovations so that they do not reach the market, they commit procrastination of innovation. Companies that want to maintain their outdated production methods or products even though more innovative production methods or products are available and affordable are committing procrastination of innovation. Investors who invest in outdated production methods or products in order to earn a return on their investment are committing procrastination of innovation.

Outdated production methods or products must be detrimental to health, the environment and living standards in order for their retention to trigger societal damage, which the law of procrastination of innovation is designed to prevent.

Entrepreneurs who commit procrastination of innovation will

117 Ministry of Innovation - 7.2 Industrial property rights
118 Ministry of Innovation - 10.3.5 People's Innovation Company Fund

be pointed out by the Company Auditing Agency's legality auditors[119] and will be penalised if they fail to rectify their deficiencies. To avoid a sentence, the companies must import the innovations immediately. All profits of the company must be used for this purpose until the innovation is introduced. Any other use of the profits, such as wage increases and dividends, is not permitted until that time. After that time, the company must pay 1% of its annual profits over 25 years as a penalty payment to the Innovation Fund .[120]

Persons who intentionally commit procrastination of innovation in contravention of the Company Auditing Agency's deficiency notices will be liable to a fine or imprisonment. The monetary value is measured by the damage caused to society. Offenders are liable first with the company's assets, then with their private assets in the form of a fine. The residual value over and above this is the term of imprisonment. Those who delay innovations, thereby damaging generations in the future, must expect imprisonment until they die.

8.10 Ministry of Integration

8.10.1 Identity cards

Every person must carry a valid identity card when in public. The police are entitled to inspect the identity cards of persons who are in public at any time. The same applies to driving licences when driving motorised vehicles and aircraft. Those who cannot identify themselves must pay a monetary fine of 50 Dollars.

8.10.2 Departure

Foreigners are obliged to depart on the date they have given to the Integration Agency.[121] If the quota of foreigners has been reached, the Integration Agency can also initiate the

---

119 Ministry of Labour - 20.7.6.10 Enforcement of innovation law
120 Ministry of Innovation - 9.11.1.1 Innovation Fund
121 Ministry of Integration - 4.2.2 Guest

obligation to depart.[122] Refugees and asylum seekers have the obligation to depart after their country of origin has been classified as safe by the Ministry of Foreign Affairs or the Integration Agency deports them.[123] If they do not do so, they commit a criminal offence and are put on the wanted list. The offence can be punished with a monetary fine, detention or deportation. Short time limits are punishable by monetary fines, longer ones are punishable by detention equal to the time limit. If foreigners cannot pay for their departure, they are deported after having developed the costs of deportation in detention.

8.10.3 Expired visa

Visas have a time limit during which they are valid. The departure must take place by the expiry of the deadline at the latest.[124] If the visa is overstayed by one week after the expiry date, a detention order will be issued. For each day of overstay, one day in detention is due. After that, deportation will take place. If the deportation fees cannot be paid by the originators, the amount must be developed in an extended imprisonment before deportation.

8.10.4 Deportations[125]

Domestic citizens cannot be deported from the inland. They may be extradited to the foreigner who has filed an extradition request with the embassy in that foreign country, which must be approved by a domestic court on the basis of a convicted offence. Foreigners who endanger the security of the population are deported.[126] As soon as a foreigner is sentenced to imprisonment for a criminal offence or if he receives 3 convictions without imprisonment, he will be deported after

122 Ministry of Integration - 7.4 Quota of foreigners
123 Ministry of Integration - 8.7 Departure
124 Ministry of Foreign Affairs - 4.7.3.4 Visa
125 §24,1-4 Protection against expulsion, extradition and deportation: BV Art.25, §243,2-6 Legislation on foreigners and asylum: BV Art. 121
126 Ministry of Foreign Affairs - 4.7.3.6 Deportations, Ministry of Integration - 7.9.3 Deportation

the sentence. Whether the foreigner is a refugee, asylum seeker, naturalised, traveller, guest worker or guest does not affect the sentence and in no case saves him from deportation. The sentence consists of imprisonment to atone for the offence and to cover the costs of deportation, as well as a life ban on entering the domestic territory. Foreigners can reduce their term of imprisonment by the share for the costs of deportation if they bear the costs themselves.

Criminal foreigners who are not yet of age of majority and would receive an imprisonment under adult criminal law are immediately deported together with their entire family, consisting of parents and minor siblings.

8.10.5 Disregard of the entry ban

The first-time disregard of the entry ban is punished by an imprisonment of 5 years, after which the person is deported again. Repeated disregard of the entry ban is punishable by an imprisonment of 10 years, after which the person is deported again.

8.10.6 Sects

Cults are prohibited. Cults are religious communities that have exclusive admission for selected members and lack constitutional fidelity. If a cult is nevertheless discovered, it is dissolved by imposing a monetary fine or community service on members, imprisoning cult leaders for at least 3 years, and confiscating premises, assets and equipment.

8.10.7 Religious crimes

Crimes that are justified on the basis of religion are punished more severely. Affected religious associations have to prove that they do not radicalise their members in an anti-constitutional way. If crimes repeatedly occur that are justified with the same religion, this religion will be banned. The dissolution of a religion in the country is carried out by giving preachers occupational bans, expropriating and selling premises, assets and equipment. Members, or practising believers, can be sentenced to community service or detention if further offences are committed in the name of the religion after the ban.

8.10.8 Incitement of the people

Anyone who preaches hatred, one-sided politicisation, calls for extremism, terrorism or other politically motivated crime commits incitement of the people. Inciters are punished with 160 community service hours for a first offence in front of an audience of less than 1000 people. Repeated offences are punishable by imprisonment for at least 12 months. Preachers who are commercially or religiously active are also banned from occupational ban.

8.11 Ministry of Justice

8.11.1 Liability

The Ministry of Justice regulates in the law of detention who is liable for damage. Persons are liable for damage for which they are at fault. They are liable with their private assets, unless the liability is covered by a detention insurance.[127] Entrepreneurs are liable for damage caused by persons or machines in their service or caused by products of the company. They are liable with their company assets, unless they have appropriate detention insurance. For their part, the ministries for economic affairs may establish liability and offer liability insurance for companies. Politicians are liable for damage caused in their office. They are liable for this with their office and can also be held liable under civil law. The Ministry of State Organisation offers liability insurance for politicians.[128]

---

127 Ministry of Health - 5.12.2.1 Accident Insurance
128 Ministry of State Organisation - 4.7 Liability insurance

8.11.2 Prison law

Those who commit crimes in detention are also tried and sentenced for them. Fines are converted into imprisonment as soon as the prisoner no longer has any assets.

8.11.3 Judicial criminal law

If faults are committed in court proceedings, the rules of procedure are violated or corruption is found among lawyers or judges, the responsible lawyers and judges are held responsible. The court proceedings take place at the National Court of Justice and result in compensation payments as punishment and optionally fines, community service, occupational ban or detention.

8.11.4 Equal treatment

Equal treatment law includes anti-discrimination measures. Those who discriminate against others on the basis of their size, age, gender, origin, religion or opinion, for example by giving them less influence or paying them less in wages, can be punished by compensation payments and monetary fines. In repeated cases with many people affected, community service or imprisonment can also be imposed.

8.11.5 Mobbing

Bullying means repeatedly and collectively speaking against a person. Blasphemy means speaking badly about other humans in their absence and spreading lies or assumptions in the social environment of the affected human. A further element is that other persons take part in blaspheming against a person. The sentence for bullying varies for the participants involved. Those who have frequently blasphemed, spread harsh abuse or even become violent are punished more severely than participants who have merely remained inactive. Bullying is punished with letters of apology, compensation payments, a monetary fine, community service or detention for up to 2 weeks. Those who have also committed defamation or violent offences will be punished additionally accordingly.

8.11.6 Negative externalities

In court proceedings for the generation of negative externalities by persons or companies, the costs incurred are determined. Negative externalities always occur when someone benefits from something and causes damage to others, but does not bear the costs. The best example is environmental pollution by companies that make profits from the product but pass on the costs of waste disposal to the population by not disposing of it properly and damaging the environment.

The individual costs of repairing the damage are used to determine all costs. This includes the medical treatment of damaged persons, damage to future generations and damage to the economy as a whole through unfair competitive advantages due to the concealment of the true costs in the sales price.

Convicted persons must transfer the sum of all costs as compensation payments to the responsible court. In the case of persons, payment in instalments or settlement in detention is possible.

In the case of companies, the amounts are due immediately or the profits must be paid to the Ministry of Justice until the compensation payments have been made in full. If this is not possible, the company is partially nationalised and must pay all profits to the Ministry of Justice and is not allowed to sell any of its own assets until the costs have been paid off.

The responsible board of directors and main responsible employees have to be detained and a new board of directors is elected by the employees. If the company becomes insolvent, any proceeds from the sale of the company's assets, all machinery and real estate, are paid into the account of the Ministry of Justice until the costs of the proceedings are covered. The rest is paid out to creditors and employees.

If foreign companies are responsible for or involved in a negative external effect, corresponding motions are filed by the embassy in the affected country. The embassy submits an extradition request for the responsible persons and requests administrative assistance through police admission to evidence. If the extradition request or administrative assistance is not approved, all trade with that country is prohibited until the costs of the negative externalities have been settled.

8.12 Ministry of Media Affairs

8.12.1 Manipulation of opinion

If a medium publishes the election results before the election closes at the end of a week, it will be closed or blocked.

Anyone who pretends to opinions by one-sided reporting or by creating artificial senders of their excessive advocacy is liable to prosecution. Possible sentences include deletion of content and senders, apology letter, monetary fine, community service or occupational ban. For media organisations, corporate criminal law also applies.

Persons and companies who are responsible for the misuse of the data will receive at least 5 years' detention.

8.12.2 False reports

Anyone who spreads false reports, passes off conjectures as facts or does inadequate source work is liable to prosecution. The sentence is a retraction at the same place of broadcasting and in the same temporal or spatial scope as the false report. In addition, a monetary fine, community service or occupational ban may be imposed. For media organisations, corporate criminal law also applies.

8.12.3 Biased reporting

As soon as journalists take sides in a report and do not mention the other points of view that speak against them or portray them badly, they can be sentenced to up to 5 years' detention and an occupational ban inland.

8.13 Ministry of Security

8.13.1 Administrative offences

The Ministry of Security issues the laws on administrative offences and, in voting with the affected ministries, the law on administrative offences in subsidiary laws. Administrative offences are warned once and the personal details of the person warned are recorded in a file. Repeated offences result in a monetary fine. If the offence is repeated three times or more, court proceedings are initiated and, if convicted, the offender is punished with community service or detention.

8.13.2 Arms industry

The manufacture of weapons of war is prohibited for all companies of all economic forms inland. Weapons of war are any weapons, projectiles or explosive devices capable of killing humans. Production sites of domestic weapons manufacturers inland are not permitted, nor is the sale of weapons production facilities. Persons who violate this are punished with at least 5 years' detention, and companies are expropriated and closed down.

Excluded from this are war weapons produced by Planned Enterprises[129] on behalf of the Ministry of Security. The Ministry of Security is allowed to sell weapons to partner countries as part of the Defence Force. Any purchases of weapons of war by the Ministry of Security must be approved by the people through voting.

It is permissible for the domestic arms industry to convert its operations to civilian use and to resume arms production only when the Ministry of Security purchases new arms.

---

129 Ministry of Planned Economy - 10.5.2 State orders

8.13.3 Duty of security agencies to provide information[130]

Security agencies have a duty to provide information to persons being dealt with by the security agencies, unless the security agencies are investigating undercover. Anyone who fails to give his or her service number or gives it incorrectly is liable to up to 12 months' detention. Anyone who fails to state the legal basis of their action when asked is liable to up to 24 months' detention. Whoever fails to announce his legal basis and to inform the person of his rights during coercive measures such as expulsion, searches or arrests is liable to up to 3 years' imprisonment.

8.13.4 Organised crime

Criminal law combats gang-related crime with imprisonment and confiscation. Anyone who illegally traffics in weapons is liable to at least 20 years' detention. Whoever extorts is liable to at least 10 years' detention. Whoever commits predatory extortion is punished with at least 20 years' detention. Anyone who is active in a criminal organisation, i.e. does not act alone, is additionally punished with at least 20 years' detention. This sentence can be reduced if those behind it are reported. Foreigners who assist and collaborate in gang-related crime are deported immediately after serving their sentence and banned from entering the domestic territory for life. All valuables and illegal means that are part of the criminal acts are confiscated. As soon as the sentence is final, confiscated illegal means are destroyed and valuables are sold. The proceeds go into compensation payments and monetary fines. Residual amounts flow into the state treasury.

8.13.5 Triggering disasters

Persons and companies that trigger disasters are held responsible. Ignorance does not protect against sentence. In the case of accidents by private individuals, a distinction is made between oversight and intent. Accidental acts only result

---

130§10.1 Protection of privacy: BV Art.13

in a fine, while intentional acts always result in imprisonment. Companies must be insured against accidents. If the insurance no longer covers the amount of damage, the company must be liable until it is insolvent. If insolvency is foreseeable on the basis of the amount of damage, the company is expropriated without compensation to the owners, nationalised and the profits transferred until all damage has been eliminated or compensated. After that, the company is sold. All owners of these companies, must be in detention. The higher the co-responsibility, the longer the imprisonment. The co-responsibility is calculated on the basis of the employee's knowledge and responsibility. Especially superiors who give work instructions have a special co-responsibility. All employees and especially subordinates who know about a dangerous work practice but do not report it to the Ministry of Security always bear joint responsibility. Employees who did not come into contact with the hazardous work practice, nor were they able to experience it, do not bear joint responsibility. Co-owners always bear joint responsibility because they have to know how they earn their money. They have a duty to inform. This applies to all companies that produce, provide services, trade or offer their goods here inland. Joint-stock companies must name all their shareholders, for whom the public prosecutor's office then issues an international arrest warrant. If naming is not possible, the shareholders are simply expropriated, which precludes further dividend payments and makes the shares worthless.

8.13.6 Violence against security forces

Anyone who uses verbal violence or at least one act of physical violence against security forces is liable to at least 6 months' detention. Security forces have the right to defend themselves against verbal and physical violence with non-lethal weapons. This defence is intended to render attackers incapable of continuing to use force, but preferably not to injure them permanently.

8.13.7 Riot

Anyone who wilfully damages persons or other people's property during a demonstration is liable to detention. The duration of the imprisonment depends on the damage caused. Anyone who damages other people's property can also be sentenced to help repair it free of charge. In this case, the owner is authorised to give instructions. The estimated working time must be proportionate to the repair work.

8.13.8 Unconstitutional behaviour of the military

Orders that violate the Constitution must be reported immediately to the Public Prosecutor's Office at the Remit Court of the Ministry of Security by any soldier who learns of or receives the orders. If there is indeed a violation of the law, charges are brought by the second instance and the responsible superiors are informed and warned to immediately put an end to this unlawful state of affairs and to immediately release the accused from service at the weapon. In the case of unconstitutional orders, there is always imminent danger, which is why expertise from the second instance must immediately bring the case before the judge. Anyone who gives unconstitutional orders or commits crimes as a soldier is punished with occupational ban and, in the case of damage to humans, also with detention.

8.13.9 War crimes

Members of the armed forces commit war crimes if they unnecessarily damage civilians, property or humanitarian organisations and operations during war, use prohibited means or improper methods of warfare. The peoples regulate violations in the International Criminal Code.[131] War criminals are punished by detention, which lasts until all their victims have been compensated. If the acts also violate applicable criminal law, these punitive measures are additionally applied.

---

131 https://www.gesetze-im-internet.de/vstgb/

8.14 Ministry of State Organisation

8.14.1 Violation of the obligation to vote

Voting in constitutional referendums is compulsory.[132] If the voting obligation is violated, one community service hour is imposed as a sentence for each missed constitutional referendum. The sentences are booked to a time account. For every 8 community service hours accumulated, one day must be spent working in a Social Village or other Non-profit institution that has reported to the town hall for community service.

8.14.2 Abuse of office[133]

The Ministry of State Organisation is responsible for legislation in general state law[134] and for the constitutional articles describing the constitutional law of state organisation[135] . State employees and politicians must comply with these state law procedures of state law. If they do not, they commit abuse of office.

The Ministry of State Organisation monitors compliance by ministries with the help of the Internal Service from the Federal Moderator's Office[136] . The External Service of the Federal Moderator's Office receives complaints from citizens and investigates the allegations itself or with the help of the Surveillance Television[137] , if undercover investigations are necessary. The audit services continuously check all state activities, including for abuse of office.[138] Each auditing agency files an abuse of office complaint with the Public Prosecutor's Office of the National Court of Justice if it suspects violations. The measures are intensified the more the alleged violation

132 Ministry of State Organisation - 9.11.5.1 Compulsory voting in constitutional referendums
133 §105.2 Liability for government decisions
134 Ministry of State Organisation - 4 State law
135 Ministry of State Organisation - 9.11 Constitutional Amendments
136 Ministry of State Organisation - 4.4 Federal Moderator's Office
137 Ministry of Media Affairs - 12.1 Monitoring team
138 Ministries of media, security, justice, finance, labour, state organisation - 2.1.2.1 Audit services

is confirmed. The first measure is that responsible state employees are informed to check whether a violation has occurred and, if so, to remedy it. These activities must be published in an accountability report. If the accountability report shows damage to individuals or the population, or if the accountability report raises more questions, investigations are launched. Investigations are the second measure. They can be conducted by a committee of enquiry[139] , a control of the Surveillance Television or by the Public Prosecutor's Office of the National Court of Justice. If the investigations provide evidence of abuse of office, court proceedings are opened before the responsible Remit Court of the affected ministry, the National Court of Justice or the Constitutional Court. If the abuse of office was committed by a state employee, the Remit Court is responsible. If it was committed by a politician, the National Court of Justice is responsible. If the abuse of office was committed in breach of constitutional law, the Constitutional Court is responsible. In the case of a guilty verdict, official liability is applied.

8.14.2.1 Public liability[140]

State employees or politicians who have committed abuse of office must be liable for this. Injured parties are compensated in accordance with state liability law, in that the state pays the compensation payments from the state treasury and has the sum reimbursed in full or in part by those convicted.
Violations of the constitution and the law in the office of a state employee are punishable by a warning, dismissal, occupational ban in the state service, payment of compensation, community service or detention. Violations in the office of a politician may result from poor compliance with the constitution, the laws or the politician's own election programme. The sentences range from a new election, occupational ban from elected office, compensation payment or community service, to detention. In the new election, the convicted politician may be allowed or barred from standing again.

139 Ministry of State Organisation - 12.5.2 Committee of enquiry
140 §64 Public liability: BV Art.146, KV Art.71

Depending on how serious the guilt is, the sentence is harsher or lighter. Once a politician or a state employee is convicted of abuse of office, the next offence, even if minor, must carry a higher official liability.

8.14.2.2 Disregard for the will of the people

If an elected politician does not do what he promised in his programme from the election, he commits fraudulent deception on the people and is liable to 2 to 5 years' detention. All campaign statements and programme items are subject to scrutiny, especially the stated time horizons by when an election promise is to be implemented.

Anyone working in a ministry that must be degraded by popular empowerment is liable to 2 to 10 years' detention.

8.14.3 Bribery of state employees[141]

Anyone who tries to bribe state employees is liable to detention for the amount of the bribe. To do so, the state employee must report the attempted bribe and document the handover with the police. State employees who take bribes can be reported to the police. The police will conduct an undercover investigation to prove the bribe.

If state employees take a bribe or demand a bribe, they are liable to detention for the amount of the bribe and are banned from state service for life.

8.14.4 Non-transparent lobbying[142]

The criminal law fight against corruption crime is initiated by reports from the state audit services and denunciations from citizens. If politicians meet with lobbyists on official business and these conversations are not broadcast unabridged on state television, all participants face imprisonment. For politicians, this crime also results in immediate removal from office. The

---

141 §66.1 Prohibition of corruption
142 §65.5 Prohibition of instruction: BV Art.161

party of the ministry provides a deputy for the office of the imprisoned politician until a new election is held within three months. The imprisonment is up to 10 years for politicians and up to 5 years for lobbyists.

8.14.5 State Protection Criminal Law[143]

The State Protection Criminal Law applies to all proceedings before the National Court of Justice initiated as a result of an offence against the state committed by state employees, politicians or groups of citizens.[144] Investigations are carried out by the Public Prosecutor's Office of the National Court of Justice in cooperation with monitoring teams of the Surveillance Television.

8.14.5.1 Arbitrary rule

Once citizens report arbitrary rule by politicians or ministry staff, that state agency is visited by the Surveillance Television monitoring team[145] and all necessary documents are seized. The complaint can be filed with the Federal Moderator's Office, police stations, courts and the Surveillance Television. All employees are required to report the complaint immediately to all other agencies mentioned. Court proceedings will be opened at the Remit Court for State Organisation.
If arbitrary rule is proven, there is a life-long occupational ban on all state service.

8.14.5.2 Revolt

Anyone involved in revolts receives an imprisonment equal to the damage caused. The population's sense of security through revolt is punishable by up to 2 years' detention. Leaders of a revolt are liable to an additional 5 years' detention.

---

143 §105.2 Liability for government decisions
144 Ministry of State Organisation - 12 State Security
145 Ministry of Media - 12 Surveillance Television

8.14.5.3 Coup

As soon as persons or a group of persons who are not politicians or state employees attempt to take over the governance of a municipality or the entire national territory, whether by force of arms, election manipulation or opinion manipulation, this is considered a coup. The same sentences follow as for a coup d'état.

8.14.5.4 Coup d'état

As soon as politicians or other state employees illegally try to take over the governance, be it by force of arms, election manipulation or media manipulation, it is considered a coup d'état. All participants are banned from all state service for life. Leaders of a coup d'état are liable to 25 years' detention. Followers of the leader are liable to 10 years' detention. If humans have been killed, harsher imprisonments are handed down. Leaders of a coup d'état are then sentenced to life imprisonment. Armed insurgents face an imprisonment of 20 years. Unarmed insurgents involved in election rigging face an imprisonment of 10 years. Their leaders are liable to 20 years' detention.

8.15 Ministry of Barter Economy

8.15.1 Pollution in the Barter Economy

Anyone who imports non-naturally degradable items into the Barter Economy Zone[146] and uses them there will be punished with a monetary fine for the first offence. On the second offence, community service is imposed and on the third offence, the offender must leave the Barter Economy Zone and is banned from living in any Barter Economy Zone for 10 years. If the offender then commits another offence, a lifetime ban from any Barter Economy Zone will be imposed.

146Ministry of Barter Economy - 6 Barter Economy Zone

8.16 Ministry of Planned Economy

8.16.1 Social law

The Ministry of Planned Economy pursues consumer policy in the social sector by ensuring and reviewing social services[147]. If social benefits prescribed by social law are not provided or are provided inadequately, affected persons have the possibility of appealing to the Social Courts, which are represented by the Departments of Planned Economy in the Remit Courts. Denied social benefits must be granted immediately after the judgement. The judge may stipulate compensation payments to the affected person in the judgement, provided that damage has demonstrably occurred.

8.16.2 Social fraud

Social fraud is committed by anyone who unjustifiably receives social welfare.[148] This concerns the person who does not pay the Social Service even though they would have enough money to move to Planned Economy on their own, or does not declare and pay taxes on their assets appropriately. Foreigners commit social fraud by receiving social benefits through the Social Emergency Service or in the Social Villages. Those who commit social fraud are punished with compensation payments, community service and, in serious cases, detention. Foreigners are also deported and banned from entering the country for life.

8.16.3 Nepotism

Anyone who falsely accounts for working hours or favours certain persons is liable to prosecution. If this service offence occurs for the first time, it is punished with overtime of at least 50 working hours. The second time, a penalty of at least 100 working hours is due, which must be performed in all activities that are most unpopular among all Social Villagers. The third

147 Ministry of Planned Economy - 17.1 Social welfare
148 Ministry of Planned Economy - 17.1 Social welfare

time, or proven regular violation of service regulations, an imprisonment of at least 7 days is imposed.

8.16.4 Favouritism

Anyone who requests working hours in the work area basic supply[149] without needing them will receive a sentence of 50 working hours. Anyone who repeatedly requests working hours without needing them and thus wants to finance laziness will receive an imprisonment of up to 2 years. In less severe cases and rare repetitions, the sentence can also be served in additional compulsory working hours .[150]

8.16.5 Blasphemy

Blasphemy means speaking badly about other humans in their absence and spreading lies or assumptions in the social environment of the affected human. Anyone who repeatedly blasphemes in the Social Village receives additional working hours in the work area luxury supply[151] without remuneration. Whoever then blasphemes again will also receive a criminal charge for mobbing.

8.17 Ministry of Social Market Economy

8.17.1 Corporate criminal law of the Social Market Economy

Social Market Economy companies are subject to special law requirements. If they violate these requirements, they are punished under corporate criminal law. The social damage is transferred to all entrepreneurs, employees, customers and investors of the Social Market Economy in order to measure the damage. The loss of confidence in the Social Market Economy that occurs when companies do not comply with

---

149 Ministry of Planned Economy - 9 Work area basic supply
150 Ministry of Planned Economy - 9.3.4 Compulsory working hours
151 Ministry of Planned Economy - 10 Work area luxury supply

the requirements increases the sentences.

8.18 Ministry of Free Market Economy

8.18.1 Visa overstay for guest workers

The legality auditors[152] check companies for foreigners requiring visas and report them to the Ministry of Integration. If guest workers do not leave the country on time by the expiry date of their visa, they are deported. The costs are paid by the Free Market Economy company where they were employed. If a failure to do so can be detected, the company is additionally penalised under corporate criminal law.

9 Switching to the new system

The Ministry of Justice is responsible for ensuring legal certainty during the transition phase despite the restructuring of many areas of law. It regulates which norms are given a transitional period upon introduction and which norms are immediately suspended as soon as the new norm has been approved by a majority in a voting or formulated by the respective minister.

The Ministry of Justice will only take over criminal legislation, which would involve too many ministries, and legislation for jurisprudence, administration of justice and the penitentiary system. The courts and prisons will continue to operate, but the prisons will be rebuilt. Judges, prosecutors, assessors and guards will continue to be employed and transferred to their new areas of operation.

9.1 Foundation of the legal expenses insurance

The Ministry of Justice builds up or buys a legal protection insurance company. The model or object of purchase is a domestic legal protection insurance company that has existed for a long time, has satisfied employees and customers and

---

152Ministry of Labour - 20.7.6 Legality auditor

is profitable. In order to build up legal protection insurance, those Ministry of Justice employees who are tasked with building up legal protection insurance are sent to existing legal protection insurance companies for internships. After the internships, facts and statistics are compiled to create the best possible business concept.

9.2 Division of the laws

All existing laws are divided between the responsible ministries and, if necessary, also split up. For all laws where this is not possible, responsibility falls to the Ministry of Justice. The Civil Code (BGB)[153] primarily forms civil law, the Criminal Code (StGB)[154] criminal law. Public law with all the appropriate laws becomes part of the state law for the new state system. The existing constitution is gradually dismantled and the new constitution is gradually built up. During this transitional phase, in which the constitution has not yet been voted on by a majority of the people, the old constitution applies. Exceptions are permitted, except for fundamental and human rights. The new constitution forms the future constitutional law.

9.3 Abolition of the suspended sentence

The suspended sentence is abolished, as is probation. Instead, community service or shorter imprisonments are imposed.

9.4 Judicial control

Cameras will be installed in all courtrooms to allow those entitled to vote to control the justice system and elected judges.

---

153 https://www.gesetze-im-internet.de/englisch_bgb/index.html
154 https://www.gesetze-im-internet.de/englisch_stgb/index.html

9.5 Election of the judges

All sitting judges must stand for election one after the other and be confirmed in office by a majority vote of the citizens who fall within their sphere of influence. During the election campaign, they are required to cite court judgments they have handed down and of which they are proud. Judges who are not approved by a majority are dismissed. State service law does not apply, so dismissal is possible.

9.6 Reallocation of the courts

Municipal Courts are the first instance and replace the District Courts and all other Courts of First Instance. Remit Courts are the second instance and replace the Regional Courts and Higher Regional Courts. The National Court of Justice is the third instance and replaces the courts for the state administration and the Court of Justice as the supreme court. The Constitutional Court is the fourth instance and replaces the existing Constitutional Court.

9.7 Changes in detention

Prisoners no longer have to pay social security because all these insurance benefits are provided by Planned Economy. The prisons are gradually being altered. In the beginning, prisoners do contract work in the prisons. After that, only serious criminals work in the prisons, the other prisoners are driven to their workplaces by shuttle buses and wear electronic ankle bracelets. The ankle cuffs will be replaced by the collars as soon as they are operational. Once the mobile prisons are operational, the prisons are converted into hospitals or sold.

9.8 Conversion of the old ministries

For the conversion of the old ministries, all departments and units of the old ministries that are changing to this ministry are identified. The organigrams are used to determine whether an entire department and all its units are changing or only individual units. All unsuitable departments and units are dropped. The existing staff adapts its tasks to the new requirements.

Contact form

Dear reader

If you would like to make what you have read come true, in whole or in part, together with other like-minded people, I offer you several possibilities with this contact form. Fill it out, tear out the page and send it by post to:

Andreas Seidl, P.O. Box 1206, 63488 Seligenstadt / Germany

Or send the details to:

Phone: 0049 1522 818 2243 (whatsapp, telegram, signal)

Email: andreas.seidl2022@web.de

Please mark with a cross:

O   I want to found a dynamic People's Party.

O   I want to donate money for implementation.

O   I want contacts with like-minded people in my area.

Forename: _____

Surname: _____

Please fill in only the contact option through which a reply should be made.

Street, house no.:   _____

Postcode, city, country: _____

Phone: _____

Email address: _____